AN INT[illegible]ON

TO

SPANISH VERBS

and how to use them.

Collected and presented by Adrian R. Leath.

One hundred Spanish verbs (or 166 English ones) declined in five tenses.

Plus a dictionary of almost 3500 English verbs with their Spanish equivalents.

Published by the Author
Adrian R. Leath
10 Arrow Industrial Estate
Eelmoor Road, Farnborough
Hampshire, GU14 7QN

Printed by
The Greywell Press
Tel. No. (0252) 544221

ISBN 0 9514327 0 2

INDEX:

Index of the declined verbs:

Before taking up residence in Spain I was convinced that I would be speaking the language fluently within a year or so. How wrong I was! By that time I knew an awful lot of words but still had great difficulty in expressing myself. I eventually realised that the key to the language was the verbs, knowing them and how to use them. I also realised that this was the major stumbling block for most English people.

I then embarked upon a six months course of instruction and during this time I learned a lot about verbs. In some ways I learned too much about verbs because at the end of that time I was still having difficulty remembering how to say very simple things. In short, I learned **about** verbs but not how to make simple, everyday use of them.

The purpose of this book (apart from fitting into your pocket) is to help the beginner to avoid the frustrating time that I myself spent before I could say "Did'nt I see you on the beach yesterday?"

A verb is of course a word that expresses an action, a doing word. All Spanish verbs in their pure form end in either ar, er or ir. These endings change according to who is doing the thing and in which tense we are speaking. These changes occur to set rules although in some cases there are variations of the rules, these are the irregular verbs.

Unfortunately a large number of the most important and common verbs **are** irregular and for this reason I intend to set them out as simply as possible for you.

If you remove the ending of the verb, that is the ar, er or ir, the part that you are left with is known as the "stem". Some verbs also have stem changes.

There are in fact no less than fifteen tenses or modes of verbs in the Spanish language and I know many Spanish people who are completely un-aware of the existance of some of them and yet they get by!

I have therefore chosen the five most important and basic tenses for *you* to be able to communicate in the Spanish language and I would suggest that if you can master these you will be well on the way.

Notes on the Spanish alphabet and pronunciation.

The Spanish alphabet contains three different letters or symbols that we do not have.
The first one CH, comes after C in their alphabet and is pronounced as we would normally pronounce this combination, as in cheese.

The second, LL which comes after L in the alphabet, when forming the start of a word is sometimes pronounced as we pronounce the letter J and sometimes as Y. With the verbs **LLEVAR** (to carry or wear) and **LLOVER** (to rain) it is pronounced as J and with the verbs **LLEGAR** (to arrive), **LLAMAR** (to call), **LLORAR** (to cry) and **LLENAR** (to fill) it is pronounced as Y.
The third, Ñ, which comes after N in the alphabet is always pronounced the same way, i.e. as we would pronounce the NY in canyon. Most people will be familiar with this pronounciation from the words señor and mañana.

Generally speaking, Spanish pronunciation is not difficult as most of the letters always retain the same pronunciation, which is more than can be said for English. Also, many have the same pronunciation as in English, the exceptions are as follows:-
B is sometimes pronounced as B and sometimes as V but if you stick to pronouncing B as B and V as V you will be understood.
C is sometimes hard as the C in the English word core and in the Spanish verb **CORRER** (to run) and sometimes it is lisped to sound like TH as with the verb **CERRAR** (to close). The ruling here is that when the C is followed by A, O or U it is hard and when followed by E or I it is lisped.
G has a similar ruling, when it is followed by A, O or U it is hard as the G in go and in the Spanish verb **GOZAR** (to enjoy). When followed by E or I the G is pronounced as we would pronounce H as in the word hen. When the G is followed by U we get the sound of the GW in the name Gwen.
H is easy, it is always silent. So if you normally drop your H's, continue to do so!
J is almost always pronounced as we pronounce H and most people will be familiar with this from the names José and Juan and so it is with the verb **JUGAR** (to play), but when it is found part way through a word it is pronounced as we would pronounce the letter K i.e. as in **ROJO** (red) and **VIAJAR** (to travel).
Q, as in English is always followed by a U but the U is silent, so the Q is pronounced as we would normally pronounce the letter K in kept and thus it is with the verb **QUERER** (to want).
R. Scotsmen will have no difficulty with the Spanish pronunciation of this letter, try to roll it the way they do.
U, except when used with G or Q is pronounced as we pronounce the OO in moo.
V. - see B.
W is not part of the Spanish alphabet.
X and Y are more or less as we use them.
Z is also lisped as we would pronounce TH.

Dedication

I dedicate this book to all my fellow country-men and women who are struggling to make themselves understood in Spanish.

Subject Pronouns

SINGULAR: I — **yo**
You — (familiar) — **tú**
You — (formal) — **Usted**
He — **él**
She — **ella**
It — (masculine) — **él**
It — (feminine) — **ella**

PLUR: We — (masculine or mixed company) — **nosotros**
We — (feminine) — **nosotras**
You — (familiar, masculine or mixed company) — **vosotros**
You — (familiar, feminine) — **vosotras**
You — (formal) — **Ustedes**
They — (masculine or mixed) — **ellos**
They — (feminine) — **ellas**

Subject pronouns are not always used in conjunction with the verbs, when they are it is to add clarity or emphasis.

Where they **are** commonly used I have added them, where they are not I have omitted them.

In English we use them all the time so if you feel more comfortable putting them in, put them in!

The familiar and the formal.

Another minor complication for we English is that in Spanish there are two ways of addressing people.

Children, young people, members of our family, close friends and lovers we can be familiar with, we use tú and vosotros. Strangers, superiors and anyone that you do not wish to be familiar with you can address formally; i.e. Usted and Ustedes.

Accent and Stress

You will see that some Spanish words have an accent over one of the letters, i.e. estábamos. This is to tell you which letter to stress when you are saying a word. If we were doing the same thing in English we would have revólver, déstiny and enlíst.

To Be or not To Be.

One of the first problems that we encounter when learning the Spanish verbs is that they have two verbs for our one verb to be.

The first one is ser and this is used to describe a permanent or long term state of being, for instance "I am English" — "**Soy** inglés" or "You are pretty" — "Tú **eres** bonita".

The second one is estar, which denotes a temporary state, for instance "I am sick" — "**Estoy** enfermo" or "You are here" — "Tu **estás** aquí".

Ser is also used when counting or telling the time, "There are four of us" — "**Somos** cuatro" or "It is two o'clock" — "**Son** las dos".

Although estar denotes a temporary state of being, just to confuse you, it is also used to denote place, for instance "London is in England" — "Londres **está** en Inglaterra" or "Their homes are in the country" — "Sus casas **están** en el campo".

To Ache or To Hurt - **Doler**
(Dol-air)

Present

SING. I ache, I do ache *or* I am aching - **duelo**
You ache, you do ache *or* you are aching - **dueles** (fam.), - **Usted duele** (form.)
He/she/it aches, he/she/it does ache *or* he/she/it is aching - **duele**

PLUR. We ache, we do ache *or* we are aching - **dolemos**
You ache, you do ache *or* you are aching - **doléis** (fam.), - **Ustedes duelen** (form.)
They ache, they do ache *or* they are aching - **duelen**

Future

SING. I shall ache - **doleré**
You will ache - **delerás** (fam.), - **Usted dolerá** (form.)
He/she/it will ache - **dolerá**

PLUR We shall ache - **doleremos**
You will ache - **doleréis** (fam.), - **Ustedes dolerán** (form.)
They will ache - **dolerán**

Past (Preterit):

SING. I ached *or* I did ache - **dolí**
You ached *or* you did ache - **doliste** (fam.), - **Usted dolió** (form.)
He/she/it ached *or* he/she/it did ache - **dolió**

PLUR. We ached *or* we did ache - **dolimos**
You ached *or* you did ache - **dolisteis** (fam.), - **Ustedes dolieron** (form.)
They ached *or* they did ache - **dolieron**

Past (Indefinite)

SING. I have ached - **he dolido**
You have ached - **has dolido** (fam.), - **Usted ha dolido** (form.)
He/she/it has ached - **ha dolido**

PLUR. We have ached - **hemos dolido**
You have ached - **habéis dolido** (fam.), - **Ustedes han dolido** (form.)
They have ached - **han dolido**

Past (Imperfect or Continuous)

SING. I was aching *or* I used to ache - **dolía**
You were aching *or* you used to ache - **dolías** (fam.), - **Usted dolía** (form.)
He/she/it was aching *or* he/she/it used to ache - **dolía**

PLUR. We were aching *or* we used to ache - **dolíamos**
You were aching *or* you used to ache - **dolíais** (fam.), - **Ustedes dolían** (form.)
They were aching *or* they used to ache - **dolían**

Gerund

Aching *or* hurting - **doliendo**

To Agree - **Acordar**

Present

SING. I agree, I do agree *or* I am agreeing - **acuerdo**
You agree, you do agree *or* you are agreeing - **acuerdas** (fam.), - **Usted acuerda** (form.)
He/she/it agrees, he/she/it does agree *or* he/she/it is agreeing - **acuerda**

PLUR. We agree, we do agree *or* we are agreeing - **acordamos**
You agree, you do agree *or* you are agreeing - **acordáis** (fam.), - **Ustedes acuerdan** (form.)
They agree, they do agree *or* they are agreeing - **acuerdan**

Future

SING. I shall agree - **acordaré**
You will agree - **acordarás** (fam.), - **Usted acordará** (form.)
He/she/it will agree- **acordará**

PLUR. We shall agree - **acordaremos**
You will agree - **acordaréis** (fam.), - **Ustedes acordarán** (form.)
They will agree - **acordarán**

Past (Preterit)

SING. I agreed *or* I did agree - **acordé**
You agreed *or* you did agree - **acordaste** (fam.), - **Usted acordó** (form.)
He/she/it agreed *or* he/she/it did agree - **acordó**

PLUR. We agreed *or* we did agree - **acordamos**
You agreed *or* you did agree - **acordasteis** (fam.), - **Ustedes acordaron** (form.)
They agreed *or* they did agree - **acordaron**

Past (Indefinite)

SING I have agreed - **he acordado**
You have agreed - **has acordado** (fam.), - **Usted ha acordado** (form.)
He/she/it has agreed - **ha acordado**

PLUR. We have agreed - **hemos acordado**
You have agreed - **habéis acordado** (fam.), - **Ustedes han acordado** (form.)
They have agreed - **han acordado**

Past (Imperfect or Continuous)

SING. I was agreeing *or* I used to agree - **acordaba**
You were agreeing *or* you used to agree - **acordabas** (fam.), - **Usted acordaba** (form.)
He/she/it was agreeing *or* he/she/it used to agree - **acordaba**

PLUR. We were agreeing *or* we used to agree - **acordábamos**
You were agreeing *or* you used to agree - **acordabais** (fam.), - **Ustedes acordaban** (form.)
They were agreeing *or* they used to agree - **acordaban**

Gerund

Agreeing - **acordando**

To Answer - **Contestar**

Present

SING. I answer, I do answer *or* I am answering - **contesto**
You answer, you do answer *or* you are answering - **contestas** (fam.), - **Usted contesta** (form.)
He/she/it answers, he/she/it does answer *or* he/she/it is answering - **contesta**

PLUR. We answer, we do answer *or* we are answering - **contestamos**
You answer, you do answer *or* you are answering - **contestáis** (fam.), - **Ustedes contestan** (form.)
They answer, they do answer *or* they are answering - **contestan**

Future

SING. I shall answer - **contestaré**
You will answer - **contestarás** (fam.), - **Usted contestará** (form.)
He/she/it will answer - **contestará**

PLUR. We shall answer - **contestaremos**
You will answer - **contestaréis** (fam.), - **Ustedes contestarán** (form.)
They will answer - **contestarán**

Past (Preterit)

SING. I answered *or* I did answer - **contesté**
You answered *or* you did answer - **contestaste** (fam.), - **Usted contestó** (form.)
He/she/it answered *or* he/she/it did answer - **contestó**

PLUR. We answered *or* we did answer - **contestamos**
You answered *or* you did answer - **contestasteis** (fam.), - **Ustedes contestaron** (form.)
They answered *or* they did answer - **contestaron**

Past (Indefinite)

SING. I have answered - **he contestado**
You have answered - **has contestado** (fam.). - **Usted ha contestado** (form.)
He/she/it has answered - **ha contestado**

PLUR. We have answered - **hemos contestado**
You have answered - **habéis contestado** (fam.), - **Ustedes han contestado** (form.)
They have answered - **han contestado**

Past (Imperfect or Continuous)

SING I was answering *or* I used to answer - **contestaba**
You were answering *or* you used to answer - **contestabas** (fam.), - **Usted contestaba** (form.)
He/she/it was answering *or* he/she/it used to answer - **contestaba**

PLUR. We were answering *or* we used to answer - **contestábamos**
You were answering *or* you used to answer - **contestabais** (fam.), - **Ustedes contestaban** (form.)
They were answering *or* they used to answer - **contestaban**

Gerund

Answering - **contestando**

To Arrange - **Arreglar**

Present

SING. I arrange, I do arrange *or* I am arranging - **arreglo**
You arrange, you do arrange *or* you are arranging - **arreglas** (fam.), - **Usted arregla** (form.)
He/she/it arranges, he/she/it does arange *or* he/she/it is arranging - **arregla**

PLUR. We arrange, we do arrange *or* we are arranging - **arreglamos**
You arrange, you do arrange *or* you are arranging - **arregláis** (fam.), - **Ustedes arreglan** (form.)
They arrange, they do arrange *or* they are arranging - **arreglan**

Future

SING. I shall arrange - **arreglaré**
You will arrange - **arreglarás** (fam.), - **Usted arreglará** (form.)
He/she/it will arrange - **arreglará**

PLUR. We shall arrange - **arreglaremos**
You will arrange - **arreglaréis** (fam.), - **Ustedes arreglarán** (form.)
They will arrange - **arreglarán**

Past (Preterit)

SING. I arranged *or* I did arrange - **arreglé**
You arranged *or* you did arrange - **arreglaste** (fam.), - **Usted arregló** (form.)
He/she/it arranged *or* he/she/it did arrange - **arregló**

PLUR. We arranged *or* we did arrange - **arreglamos**
You arranged *or* you did arrange - **arreglasteis** (fam.), - **Ustedes arreglaron** (form.)
They arranged *or* they did arrange - **arreglaron**

Past (Indefinite)

SING. I have arrange - **he arreglado**
You have arranged - **has arreglado** (fam.), - **Usted ha arreglado** (form.)
He/she/it has arranged - **ha arreglado**

PLUR. We have arranged - **hemos arreglado**
You have arranged - **habéis arreglado** (fam.), - **Ustedes han arreglado** (form.)
They have arranged - **han arreglado**

Past (Imperfect or Continuous)

SING. I was arranging *or* I used to arrange - **arreglaba**
You were arranging *or* you used to arrange - **arreglabas** (fam.), - **Usted arreglaba** (form.)
He/she/it was arranging *or* he/she/it used to arrange - **arreglaba**

PLUR. We were arranging *or* we used to arrange - **arreglábamos**
You were arranging *or* you used to arrange - **arreglabais** (fam.), - **Ustedes arreglaban** (form.)
They were arranging *or* they used to arrange - **arreglaban**

Gerund

Arranging - **arreglando**

To Arrive - **Llegar**
(Yea-gar)

Present

SING. I arrive, I do arrive *or* I am arriving - **llego**
You arrive, you do arrive *or* you are arriving - **llegas** (fam.), - **Usted llega** (form).
He/she/it arrives, he/she/it does arrive *or* he/she/it is arriving - **llega**

PLUR. We arrive, we do arrive *or* we are arriving - **llegamos**
You arrive, you do arrive *or* you are arriving - **llegáis** (fam), - **Ustedes llegan** (form.)
They arrive, they do arrive *or* they are arriving - **llegan**

Future

SING. I shall arrive - **llegaré**
You will arrive - **llegarás** (fam.), - **Usted llegará** (form.)
He/she/it will arrive - **llegará**

PLUR. We shall arrive - **llegaremos**
You will arrive - **llegaréis** (fam.), - **Ustedes llegarán** (form.)
They will arrive - **llegarán**

Past (Preterit)

SING. I arrived *or* I did arrive - **llegué**
You arrived *or* you did arrive - **llegaste** (fam.), - **Usted llegó** (form.)
He/she/it arrived *or* he/she/it did arrive - **llegó**

PLUR. We arrived *or* we did arrive - **llegamos**
You arrived *or* you did arrive - **llegasteis** (fam.), - **Ustedes llegaron** (form.)
They arrived *or* they did arrive - **llegaron**

Past (Indefinite)

SING. I have arrived - **he llegado**
You have arrived - **has llegado** (fam.), - **Usted ha llegado** (form.)
He/she/it has arrived - **ha llegado**

PLUR. We have arrived - **hemos llegado**
You have arrived - **habéis llegado** (fam.), - **Ustedes han llegado** (form.)
They have arrived - **han llegado**

Past (Imperfect or Continuous)

SING. I was arriving *or* I used to arrive - **llegaba**
You were arriving *or* you used to arrive - **llegabas** (fam.), - **Usted llegaba** (form.)
He/she/it was arriving *or* he/she/it used to arrive - **llegaba**

PLUR. We were arriving *or* we used to arrive - **llegábamos**
You were arriving *or* you used to arrive- **llegabais** (fam.), - **Ustedes llegaban** (form.)
They were arriving *or* they used to arrive - **llegaban**

Gerund

Arriving - **llegando**

To Ask - **Preguntar**
(Pray-goon-tar)
(Not to be confused with To Ask For - **Pedir)**

Present

SING. I ask, I do ask *or* I am asking - **yo pregunto**
You ask, you do ask *or* you are asking - **tú preguntas** (fam.), - **Usted pregunta** (form.)
He/she/it asks, he/she/it does ask *or* he/she/it is asking - **pregunta**

PLUR. We ask, we do ask *or* we are asking - **preguntamos**
You ask, you do ask *or* you are asking - **preguntáis** (fam.), - **Ustedes preguntan** (form.)
They ask, they do ask *or* they are asking - **preguntan**

Future

SING. I shall ask - **preguntaré**
You will ask - **preguntarás** (fam.), - **Usted preguntará** (form.)
He/she/it will ask - **preguntará**

PLUR. We shall ask - **preguntaremos**
You will ask - **preguntaréis** (fam.), - **Ustedes preguntarán** (form.)
They will ask - **preguntarán**

Past (Preterit)

SING. I asked *or* I did ask - **pregunté**
You asked *or* you did ask - **preguntaste** (fam.), - **Usted preguntó** (form.)
He/she/it asked *or* he/she/it did ask - **preguntó**

PLUR. We asked *or* we did ask - **preguntamos**
You asked *or* you did ask - **preguntasteis** (fam.), - **Ustedes preguntaron** (form.)
They asked *or* they did ask - **preguntaron**

Past (Indefinite)

SING. I have asked - **he preguntado**
You have asked - **has preguntado** (fam.), - **Usted ha preguntado** (form.)
He/she/it has asked - **ha preguntado**

PLUR. We have asked - **hemos preguntado**
You have asked - **habéis preguntado** (fam.), - **Ustedes han preguntado** (form.)
They have asked - **han preguntado**

Past (Imperfect or Continuous)

SING. I was asking *or* I used to ask - **preguntaba**
You were asking *or* you used to ask - **preguntabas** (fam.), - **Usted preguntaba** (form.)
He/she/it was asking *or* he/she/it used to ask - **preguntaba**

PLUR. We were asking *or* we used to ask - **preguntábamos**
You were asking *or* you used to ask - **preguntabais** (fam.), - **Ustedes preguntaban** (form.)
They were asking *or* they used to ask - **preguntaban**

Gerund

Asking — **preguntando**

To Ask For *or* To Request - **Pedir**

Present

SING. I request, I do request *or* I am requesting - **yo pido**
You request, you do request *or* you are requesting - **tú pides** (fam.), - **Usted pide** (form.)
He/she/it requests, he/she/it does request *or* he/she/it is requesting - **pide**

PLUR. We request, we do request *or* we are requesting - **pedimos**
You request, you do request *or* you are requesting - **pedís** (fam.), - **Ustedes piden** (form.)
They request, they do request *or* they are requesting - **piden**

Future

SING. I shall request - **pediré**
You will request - **pedirás** (fam.), - **Usted pedirá** (form.)
He/she/it will request - **pedirá**

PLUR. We shall request - **pediremos**
You will request - **pediréis** (fam.), - **Ustedes pedirán** (form.)
They will request - **pedirán**

Past (Preterit)

SING. I requested *or* I did request - **pedí**
You requested *or* you did request - **pediste** (fam.), - **Usted pidió** (form.)
He/she/it requested *or* he/she/it did request - **pidió**

PLUR. We requested *or* we did request - **pedimos**
You requested *or* you did request - **pedisteis** (fam.), - **Ustedes pidieron** (form.)
They requested *or* they did request - **pidieron**

Past (Indefinite)

SING. I have requested - **he pedido**
You have requested - **has pedido** (fam.), - **Usted ha pedido** (form.)
He/she/it has requested - **ha pedido**

PLUR. We have requested - **hemos pedido**
You have requested - **habéis pedido** (fam.), - **Ustedes han pedido** (form.)
They have requested - **han pedido**

Past (Imperfect or Continuous)

SING. I was requesting *or* I used to request - **pedía**
You were requesting *or* you used to request - **pedías** (fam.), - **Usted pedía** (form.)
He/she/it was requesting *or* he/she/it used to request - **pedía**

PLUR. We were requesting *or* we used to request - **pedíamos**
You were requesting *or* you used to request - **pedíais** (fam.), - **Ustedes pedían** (form.)
They were requesting *or* they used to request - **pedían**

Gerund

Asking for *or* requesting - **pidiendo**

To Be - **Ser**
(See "To Be or not To Be" - Page 9)

Present

SING. I am - **yo soy**
You are - **tú eres** (fam.), - **Usted es** (form.)
He/she/it is - **es**

PLUR.We are - **somos**
You are - **sois** (fam.), - **Ustedes son** (form.s)
They are - **son**

Future

SING. I shall be - **seré**
You will be - **serás** (fam.), - **Usted será** (form.)
He/she/it will be - **será**

PLUR.We shall be - **seremos**
You will be - **seréis** (fam.), - **Ustedes serán** (form.)
They will be - **serán**

Past (Preterit)

SING. I was - **fui**
You were - **fuiste** (fam.), - **Usted fue** (form.)
He/she/it was - **fue**

PLUR.We were - **fuimos**
You were - **fuisteis** (fam.), - **Ustedes fueron** (form.)
They were - **fueron**

Past (Indefinite)

SING. I have been - **he sido**
You have been - **has sido** (fam.), - **Usted ha sido** (form.)
He/she/it has been - **ha sido**

PLUR.We have been - **hemos sido**
You have been - **habéis sido** (fam.), - **Ustedes han sido** (form.)
They have been - **han sido**

Past (Imperfect or Continuous)

SING. I used to be - **era**
You used to be - **eras** (fam.), - **Usted era** (form.)
He/she/it used to be - **era**

PLUR.We used to be - **éramos**
You used to be - **erais** (fam.), - **Ustedes eran** (form.)
They used to be - **eran**

Gerund

Being - **siendo**

To Be - **Estar**
(See "To Be or not To Be - Page 9)

(See "To Be or not To Be - Page 9)

Present

SING. I am *or* I am being - **estoy**
You are *or* you are being - **estás** (fam.), - **Usted está** (form.)
He/she/it is *or* he/she/it is being - **está**

PLUR. We are *or* we are being - **estamos**
You are *or* you are being - **estáis** (fam.), - **Ustedes están** (form.)
They are *or* they are being - **están**

Future

SING. I shall be - **estaré**
You will be - **estarás** (fam.), - **Usted estará** (form.)
He/she/it will be - **estará**

PLUR. We shall be - **estaremos**
You will be - **estaréis** (fam.), - **Ustedes estarán** (form.)
They will be - **estarán**

Past (Preterit)

SING. I was - **estuve**
You were - **estuviste** (fam.), - **Usted estuvo** (form.)
He/she/it was - **estuvo**

PLUR. We were - **estuvimos**
You were - **estuvisteis** (fam.), - **Ustedes estuvieron** (form.)
They were - **estuvieron**

Past (Indefinite)

SING. I have been - **he estado**
You have been - **has estado** (fam.), - **Usted ha estado** (form.)
He/she/it has been - **ha estado**

PLUR. We have been - **hemos estado**
You have been - **habéis estado** (fam.), - **Ustedes han estado** (form.)
They have been - **han estado**

Past (Imperfect or Continuous)

SING. I was being *or* I used to be - **estaba**
You were being *or* you used to be - **estabas** (fam.). - **Usted estaba** (form.)
He/she/it was being *or* he/she/it used to be - **estaba**

PLUR. We were being *or* we used to be - **estábamos**
You were being *or* you used to be - **estabais** (fam.), - **Ustedes estaban** (form.)
They were being *or* they used to be - **estaban**

Gerund

Being - **estando**

To Be Able (Can) - **Poder**
(Po-dair)

Present

SING. I can *or* I am able to - **puedo**
You can *or* you are able to - **puedes** (fam.), - **Usted puede** (form.)
He/she/it can *or* he/she/it is able to - **puede**

PLUR. We can *or* we are able to - **podemos**
You can *or* you are able to - **podéis** (fam.), - **Ustedes pueden** (form.)
They can *or* they are able to - **pueden**

Future

SING. I shall be able to - **podré**
You will be able to - **podrás** (fam.), - **Usted podrá** (form.)
He/she/it/will be able to - **podrá**

PLUR. We shall be able to - **podremos**
You will be able to - **podréis** (fam.), - **Ustedes podrán** (form.)
They will be able to - **podrán**

Past (Preterit)

SING. I could - **pude**
You could - **pudiste** (fam.), - **Usted pudo** (form.)
He/she/it could - **pudo**

PLUR. We could - **pudimos**
You could - **pudisteis** (fam.), - **Ustedes pudieron** (form.)
They could - **pudieron**

Past (Indefinite)

SING. I have been able to - **he podido**
You have been able to - **has podido** (fam.), - **Usted ha podido** (form.)
He/she/it has been able to - **ha podido**

PLUR. We have been able to - **hemos podido**
You have been able to - **habéis podido** (fam.), - **Ustedes han podido** (form.)
They have been able to - **han podido**

Past (Imperfect or Continuous)

SING. I used to be able to - **podía**
You used to be able to - **podías** (fam.), - **Usted podía** (form.)
He/she/it used to be able to - **podía**

PLUR. We used to be able to - **podíamos**
You used to be able to - **podíais** (fam.), - **Ustedes podían** (form.)
They used to be able to - **podían**

Gerund

Being able to - **pudiendo**

To Begin - **Empezar**
(Also To Start) *(Em-peth-ar)*

Present

SING. I begin, I do begin *or* I am beginning - **yo empiezo**
You begin, you do begin *or* you are beginning - **tú empiezas** (fam.), - **Usted empieza** (form.)
He/she/it begins, he/she/it does begin *or* he/she/it is beginning - **empieza**

PLUR.We begin, we do begin *or* we are beginning - **empezamos**
You begin, you do begin *or* you are beginning - **empezáis** (fam.), - **Ustedes empiezan** - (form.)
They begin, they do begin *or* they are beginning - **empiezan**

Future

SING.I shall begin - **empezaré**
You will begin - **empezarás** (fam.), - **Usted empezará** (form.)
He/she/it will begin - **empezará**

PLUR.We shall begin - **empezaremos**
You will begin - **empezaréis** (fam.), - **Ustedes empezarán** (form.)
They will begin - **empezarán**

Past (Preterit)

SING. I began *or* I did begin - **empecé**
You began *or* you did begin - **empezaste** (fam.), - **Usted empezó** (form.)
He/she/it began *or* he/she/it did begin - **empezó**

PLUR. We began *or* we did begin - **empezamos**
You began *or* you did begin - **empezasteis** (form.), - **Ustedes empezaron** (form.)
They began *or* they did begin - **empezaron**

Past (Indefinite)

SING. I have begun - **he empazado**
You have begun - **has empezado** (fam), - **Usted ha empezado** (form.)
He/she/it has begun - **ha empezado**

PLUR.We have begun - **hemos empezado**
You have begun - **habéis empezado** (fam.), - **Ustedes han empezado** (form.)
They have begun - **han empezado**

Past (Imperfect *or* Continuous)

SING. I was beginning *or* I used to begin - **empezaba**
You were beginning *or* you used to begin - **empezabas** (fam.), - **Usted empezaba** (form.)
He/she/it was beginning *or* he/she/it used to begin - **empezaba**

PLUR. We were beginning *or* we used to begin - **empezábamos**
You were beginning *or* you used to begin - **empezabais** (fam.), - **Ustedes empezaban** (form.)
They were beginning *or* they used to begin - **empezaban**

Gerund

Beginning *or* starting - **empezando**

To Believe - **Creer**
(Cray-air)

Present

SING. I believe *or* I do believe - **creo**
You believe *or* you do believe - **crees** (fam.), - **Usted cree** (form.)
He/she/it believes *or* he/she/it does believe - **cree**

PLUR. We believe *or* we do believe - **creemos**
You believe *or* you do believe - **creéis** (fam.), - **Ustedes creen** (form.)
They believe *or* they do believe - **creen**

Future

SING. I shall believe - **creeré**
You will believe - **creerás** (fam.), - **Usted creerá** (form.)
He/she/it will believe - **creerá**

PLUR. We shall believe - **creeremos**
You will believe - **creeréis** (fam.), - **Ustedes creerán** (form.)
They will believe - **creerán**

Past (Preterit)

SING. I believed *or* I did believe - **creí**
You believed *or* you did believe - **creíste** (fam.), - **Usted creyó** (form.)
He/she/it believed *or* he/she/it did believe - **creyó**

PLUR. We believed *or* we did believe - **creímos**
You believed *or* you did believe - **creísteis** (fam.), - **Ustedes creyeron** (form.)
They believed *or* they did believe - **creyeron**

Past (Indefinite)

SING. I have believed - **he creído**
You have believed - **has creído** (fam.), - **Usted ha creído** (form.)
He/she/it has believed - **ha creído**

PLUR. We have believed - **hemos creído**
You have believed - **habéis creído** (fam.), - **Ustedes han creído** (form.)
They have believed - **han creído**

Past (Imperfect or Continuous)

SING. I used to believe - **creía**
You used to believe - **creías** (fam.), - **Usted creía** (form.)
He/she/it used to believe - **creía**

PLUR. We used to believe - **creíamos**
You used to believe - **creíais** (fam.), - **Ustedes creían** (form.)
They used to believe - **creían**

Gerund

Believing - **creyendo**

To Bring - **Traer**
(Try-air)

Present

SING. I bring, I do bring *or* I am bringing - **traigo**
You bring, you do bring *or* you are bringing - **traes** (fam.), - **Usted trae** (form.)
He/she/it brings, he/she/it does bring *or* he/she/it is bringing - **trae**

PLUR. We bring, we do bring *or* we are bringing - **traemos**
You bring, you do bring *or* you are bringing - **traéis** (fam.), - **Ustedes traen** (form.)
They bring, they do bring *or* they are bringing - **traen**

Future

SING. I shall bring - **traeré**
You will bring - **traerás** (fam.), - **Usted traerá** (form.)
He/she/it will bring - **traerá**

PLUR. We shall bring - **traeremos**
You will bring - **traeréis** (fam.), - **Ustedes traerán** (form.)
They will bring - **traerán**

Past (Preterit)

SING. I brought *or* I did bring - **traje**
You brought *or* you did bring - **trajiste** (fam.), - **Usted trajo** (form.)
He/she/it brought *or* he/she/it did bring - **trajo**

PLUR. We brought *or* we did bring - **trajimos**
You brought *or* you did bring - **trajisteis** (fam.), - **Ustedes trajeron** (form.)
They brought *or* they did bring - **trajeron**

Past (Indefinite)

SING. I have brought - **he traído**
You have brought - **has traído** (fam.), - **Usted ha traído** (form.)
He/she/it has brought - **ha traído**

PLUR. We have brought - **hemos traído**
You have brought - **habéis traído** (fam.), - **Ustedes han traído** (form.)
They have brought - **han traído**

Past (Imperfect or Continuous)

SING. I was bringing *or* I used to bring - **traía**
You were bringing *or* you used to bring - **traías** (fam.), - **Usted traía** (form.)
He/she/it was bringing *or* he/she/it used to bring - **traía**

PLUR. We were bringing *or* we used to bring - **traíamos**
You were bringing *or* you used to bring - **traíais** (fam.), **Ustedes traían** (form.)
They were bringing *or* they used to bring - **traían**

Gerund

Bringing - **trayendo**

To Buy - **Comprar**

Present

SING. I buy, I do buy *or* I am buying - **compro**
You buy, you do buy *or* you are buying - **compras** (fam.), - **Usted compra** (form.)
He/she/it buys, he/she/it does buy *or* he/she/it is buying - **compra**

PLUR. We buy, we do buy *or* we are buying - **compramos**
You buy, you do buy *or* you are buying - **compráis** (fam.), **Ustedes compran** (form.)
They buy, they do buy *or* they are buying - **compran**

Future

SING. I shall buy - **compraré**
You will buy - **comprarás** (fam.), - **Usted comprará** (form.)
He/she/it will buy - **comprará**

PLUR. We shall buy - **compraremos**
You will buy - **compraréis** (fam.), - **Ustedes comprarán** (form.)
They will buy - **comprarán**

Past (Preterit)

SING. I bought *or* I did buy - **compré**
You bought *or* you did buy - **compraste** (fam.), - **Usted compró** (form.)
He/she/it bought *or* he/she/it did buy - **compró**

PLUR. We bought *or* we did buy - **compramos**
You bought *or* you did buy - **comprasteis** (fam.), - **Ustedes compraron** (form.)
They bought *or* they did buy - **compraron**

Past (Indefinite)

SING. I have bought - **he comprado**
You have bought - **has comprado** (fam.), - **Usted ha comprado** (form.)
He/she/it has bought - **ha comprado**

PLUR. We have bought - **hemos comprado**
You have bought - **habéis comprado** (fam.), - **Ustedes han comprado** (form.)
They have bought - **han comprado**

Past (Imperfect or Continuous)

SING. I was buying *or* I used to buy - **compraba**
You were buying *or* you used to buy - **comprabas** (fam.), - **Usted compraba** (form.)
He/she/it was buying *or* he/she/it used to buy - **compraba**

PLUR. We were buying *or* we used to buy - **comprábamos**
You were buying *or* you used to buy - **comprabais** (fam.), - **Ustedes compraban** (form.)
They were buying *or* they used to buy - **compraban**

Gerund

Buying - **comprando**

To Call - **Llamar**

(Yam-ar)

Present

SING. I call, I do call *or* I am calling - **llamo**
You call, you do call *or* you are calling - **llamas** (fam.), - **Usted llama** (form.)
He/she/it calls, he/she/it does call *or* he/she/it is calling - **llama**

PLUR. We call, we do call *or* we are calling - **llamamos**
You call, you do call *or* you are calling - **llamáis** (fam.), - **Ustedes llaman** (form.)
They call, they do call *or* they are calling - **llaman**

Future

SING. I shall call - **llamaré**
You will call - **llamarás** (fam.), - **Usted llamará** (form.)
He/she/it will call - **llamará**

PLUR. We shall call - **llamaremos**
You will call - **llamaréis** (fam.), - **Ustedes llamarán** (form.)
They will call - **llamarán**

Past (Preterit)

SING. I called *or* I did call - **llamé**
You called *or* you did call - **llamaste** (fam.), - **Usted llamó** (form.)
He/she/it called *or* he/she/it did call - **llamó**

PLUR. We called *or* we did call - **llamamos**
You called *or* you did call - **llamasteis** (fam.), - **Ustedes llamaron** (form.)
They called *or* they did call - **llamaron**

Past (Indefinite)

SING. I have called - **he llamado**
You have called - **has llamado** (fam.), - **Usted ha llamado** (form.)
He/she/it has called - **ha llamado**

PLUR. We have called - **hemos llamado**
You have called - **habéis llamado** (fam.), - **Ustedes han llamado** (form.)
They have called - **han llamado**

Past (Imperfect or Continuous)

SING. I was calling *or* I used to call - **llamaba**
You were calling *or* you used to call - **llamabas** (fam.), - **Usted llamaba** (form.)
He/she/it was calling *or* he/she/it used to call - **llamaba**

PLUR. We were calling *or* we used to call - **llamábamos**
You were calling *or* you used to call - **llamabais** (fam.), - **Ustedes llamaban** (form.)
They were calling *or* they used to call - **llamaban**

Gerund

Calling - **llamando**

To Call Oneself *or* To Be Named - **Llamarse**
(Yam-ar-say)

Present

SING. I call myself *or* my name is- **me llamo**
You call yourself - **te llamas** (fam.), - **Usted se llama** (form.)
He/she calls him/herself - **se llama**
It is called - **se llama**

PLUR. We call ourselves - **nos llamamos**
You call yourselves - **òs llamáis** (fam.), - **Ustedes se llaman** (form.)
They call themselves *or* they are called - **se llaman**

Future

SING. I shall call myself - **me llamaré**
You will call yourself - **te llamarás** (fam.), - **Usted se llamará** (form.)
He/she will call him/herself - **se llamará**
It will be called - **se llamará**

PLUR.We shall call ourselves - **nos llamaremos**
You will call yourselves - **os llamaréis** (fam.), - **Ustedes se llamarán** (form.)
They will call themselves *or* they will be called - **se llamarán**

Past (Preterit)

SING. I called myself - **me llamé**
You called yourself - **te llamaste** (fam.), - **Usted se llamó** (form.)
He/she called him/herself - **se llamó**
It was called - **se llamó**

PLUR.We shall call ourselves - **nos llamaremos**
You will call yourselves - **os llamaréis** (fam.), - **Ustedes se llamarán** (form.)
They will call themselves *or* they will be called - **se llamarán**

Past (Indefinite)

SING.I have called myself - **me he llamado**
You have called yourself - **te has llamado** (fam.), - **Usted se ha llamado** (form.)
He/she/it has called him/her/itself - **se ha llamado**
It has been called - **se ha llamado**

PLUR. We have called ourselves - **nos hemos llamado**
You have called yourselves - **os habéis llamado** (fam.), - **Ustedes se han llamado** (form.)
They have called themselves *or* they have been called - **se han llamado**

Past (Imperfect *or* Continuous)

SING.I was calling myself *or* I used to call myself - **me llamaba**
You were calling yourself *or* you used to call yourself - **te llamabas** (fam.), - **Usted se llamaba** (form.)
He/she was calling him/herself *or* he/she used to call him/herself - **se llamaba**
It used to be called - **se llamaba**

PLUR
We were calling ourselves *or* we used to call ourselves - **nos llamábamos**
You were calling yourselves *or* you used to call yourselves - **os llamabais** (fam.), - **Ustedes se llamaban** (form.)
They were calling themselves, they used to call themselves *or* they used to be called - **se llamaban**

Gerund

Calling oneself *or* being named - **llamándose**

To Care For *or* To Take Care Of - **Cuidar**
(Cwee-dar)

Present

SING. I take care of *or* I am taking care of - **yo cuido**
You take care of *or* you are taking care of - **tú cuidas** (fam.), - **Usted cuida** (form.)
He/she/it takes care of *or* he/she/it is taking care of - **cuida**

PLUR. We take care of *or* we are taking care of - **cuidamos**
You take care of *or* you are taking care of - **cuidáis** (fam.), - **Ustedes cuidan** (form.)
They take care of *or* they are taking care of - **cuidan**

Future

SING. I shall take care of - **cuidaré**
You will take care of - **cuidarás** (fam.), - **Usted cuidará** (form.)
He/she/it will take care of - **cuidará**

PLUR. We shall take care of - **cuidaremos**
You will take care of - **cuidaréis** (fam.), - **Ustedes cuidarán** (form.)
They will take care of - **cuidarán**

Past (Preterit)

SING. I took care of *or* I did take care of - **cuidé**
You took care of *or* you did take care of - **cuidaste** (fam.), - **Usted cuidó** (form.)
He/she/it took care of *or*/she/it did take care of - **cuidó**

PLUR. We took care of *or* we did take care of - **cuidamos**
You took care of *or* you did take care of - **cuidasteis** (fam.), - **Ustedes cuidaron** (form.)
They took care of *or* they did take care of - **cuidaron**

Past (Indefinite)

SING. I have taken care of - **he cuidado**
You have taken care of - **has cuidado** (fam.), - **Usted ha cuidado** (form.)
He/she/it has taken care of - **ha cuidado**

PLUR. We have taken care of - **hemos cuidado**
You have taken care of - **habéis cuidado** (fam.), - **Ustedes han cuidado** (form.)
They have taken care of - **han cuidado**

Past (Imperfect or Continuous)

SING. I was taking care of *or* I used to take care of - **cuidaba**
You were taking care of *or* you used to take care of - **cuidabas** (fam.), - **Usted cuidaba** (form.)
He/she/it was taking care of *or* he/she/it used to take care of - **cuidaba**

PLUR. We were taking care of *or* we used to take care of - **cuidábamos**
You were taking care of *or* you used to take care of - **cuidabais** (fam.), - **Ustedes cuidaban** (form.)
They were taking care of *or* they used to take care of - **cuidaban**

Gerund

Taking care of - **cuidando**

To Carry - **Llevar** *(Jay - var)*
(Also to take someone by car)
(Also To Wear, but not to be confused with To Put On - **Ponerse**).

Present

SING. I carry, I do carry *or* I am carrying - **llevo**
You carry, you do carry *or* you are carrying - **llevas** (fam.), - **Usted lleva** (form.)
He/she/it carries, he/she/it does carry *or* he/she/it is carrying - **lleva**

PLUR. We carry, we do carry *or* we are carrying - **llevamos**
You carry, you do carry *or* you are carrying - **lleváis** (fam.), - **Ustedes llevan** (form.)
They carry, they do carry *or* they are carrying - **llevan**

Future

SING. I shall carry - **llevaré**
You will carry - **llevarás** (fam.), - **Usted llevará** (form.)
He/she/it will carry - **llevará**

PLUR. We shall carry - **llevaremos**
You will carry - **llevaréis** (fam.), - **Ustedes llevarán** (form.)
They will carry - **llevarán**

Past (Preterit)

SING. I carried *or* I did carry - **llevé**
You carried *or* you did carry - **llevaste** (fam.), - **Usted llevó** (form.)
He/she/it carried *or* he/she/it did carry - **llevó**

PLUR. We carried *or* we did carry - **llevamos**
You carried *or* you did carry - **llevasteis** (fam.), - **Ustedes llevaron** (form.)
They carried *or* they did carry - **llevaron**

Past (Indefinite)

SING. I have carried - **he llevado**
You have carried - **has llevado** (fam.), - **Usted ha llevado** (form.)
He/she/it has carried - **ha llevado**

PLUR. We have carried - **hemos llevado**
You have carried - **habéis llevado** (fam.), - **Ustedes han llevado** (form.)
They have carried - **han llevado**

Past (Imperfect or Continuous)

SING. I was carrying *or* I used to carry - **llevaba**
You were carrying *or* you used to carry - **llevabas** (fam.), - **Usted llevaba** (form.)
He/she/it was carrying *or* he/she/it used to carry - **llevaba**

PLUR. We were carrying *or* we used to carry - **llevábamos**
You were carrying *or* you used to carry - **llevabais** (fam.), - **Ustedes llevaban** (form.)
They were carrying *or* they used to carry - **llevaban**

Gerund

Carrying *or* Wearing - **llevando**

To Close - **Cerrar**
(Ther - rar)

Present

SING. I close, I do close *or* I am closing - **cierro**
You close, you do close *or* you are closing - **cierras** (fam.), - **Usted cierra** (form.)
He/she/it closes, he/she/it does close *or* he/she/it is closing - **cierra**

PLUR. We close, we do close *or* we are closing - **cerramos**
You close, you do close *or* you are closing - **cerráis** (fam.), - **Ustedes cierran** (form.)
They close, they do close *or* they are closing - **cierran**

Future

SING. I shall close - **cerraré**
You will close - **cerrarás** (fam.), - **Usted cerrará** (form.)
He/she/it will close - **cerrará**

PLUR. We shall close - **cerraremos**
You will close - **cerraréis** (fam.), - **Ustedes cerrarán** (form.)
They will close - **cerrarán**

Past (Preterit)

SING. I closed *or* I did close - **cerré**
You closed *or* you did close - **cerraste** (fam.), - **Usted cerró** (form.)
He/she/it closed *or* he/she/it did close - **cerró**

PLUR. We closed *or* we did close - **cerramos**
You closed *or* you did close - **cerrasteis** (fam.), - **Ustedes cerraron** (form.)
They closed *or* they did close - **cerraron**

Past (Indefinite)

SING. I have closed - **he cerrado**
You have closed - **has cerrado** (fam.), - **Usted ha cerrado** (form.)
He/she/it has closed - **ha cerrado**

PLUR. We have closed - **hemos cerrado**
You have closed - **habéis cerrado** (fam.), - **Ustedes han cerrado** (form.)
They have closed - **han cerrado**

Past (Imperfect *or* Continuous)

SING. I was closing *or* I used to close - **cerraba**
You were closing *or* you used to close - **cerrabas** (fam.), - **Usted cerraba** (form.)
He/she/it was closing *or* he/she/it used to close - **cerraba**

PLUR. We were closing *or* we used to close - **cerrábamos**
You were closing *or* you used to close - **cerrabais** (fam.), - **Ustedes cerraban** (form.)
They were closing *or* they used to close - **cerraban**

Gerund

Closing - **cerrando**

To Come - **Venir**
(Ven-ear)

Present

SING. I come, I do come *or* I am coming - **yo vengo**
You come, you do come *or* you are coming - **tú vienes** (fam.), - **Usted viene** (form.)
He/she/it comes, he/she/it does come *or* he/she/it is coming - **viene**

PLUR.We come, we do come *or* we are coming - **venimos**
You come, you do come *or* you are coming - **venís** (fam.), - **Ustedes vienen** (form.)
They come, they do come *or* they are coming - **vienen**

Future

SING. I shall come - **vendré**
You will come - **vendrás** (fam.), - **Usted vendrá** (form.)
He/she/it will come - **vendrá**

PLUR.We shall come - **vendremos**
You will come - **vendréis** (fam.), - **Ustedes vendrán** (form.)
They will come - **vendrán**

Past (Preterit)

SING. I came *or* I did come - **vine**
You came *or* you did come - **viniste** (fam.), - **Usted vino** (form.)
He/she/it came *or* he/she/it did come - **vino**

PLUR.We came *or* we did come - **vinimos**
You came *or* you did come - **vinisteis** (fam.), - **Ustedes vinieron** (form.)
They came *or* they did come - **vinieron**

Past (Indefinite)

SING. I have come - **he venido**
You have come - **has venido** (fam.), - **Usted ha venido** (form.)
He/she/it has come - **ha venido**

PLUR.We have come - **hemos venido**
You have come - **habéis venido** (fam.), - **Ustedes han venido** (form.)
They have come - **han venido**

Past (Imperfect *or* Continuous)

SING. I was coming *or* I used to come - **venía**
You were coming *or* you used to come - **venías** (fam.), - **Usted venía** (form.)
He/she/it was coming *or* he/she/it used to come - **venía**

PLUR.We were coming *or* we used to come - **veníamos**
You were coming *or* you used to come - **veníais** (fam.), - **Ustedes venían** (form.)
They were coming *or* they used to come - **venían**

Gerund

Coming - **viniendo**

To Count - **Contar**
(Also to Relate *or* Tell)

Present

SING. I count, I do count *or* I am counting - **yo cuento**
You count, you do count *or* you are counting - **tú cuentas** (fam.), - **Usted cuenta** (form.)
He/she/it counts, he/she/it does count *or* he/she/it is counting - **cuenta**

PLUR. We count, we do count *or* we are counting - **contamos**
You count, you do count *or* you are counting - **contáis** (fam.), - **Ustedes cuentan** (form.)
They count, they do count *or* they are counting - **cuentan**

Future

SING. I shall count - **contaré**
You will count - **contarás** (fam.), - **Usted contará** (form.)
He/she/it will count - **contará**

PLUR. We shall count - **contaremos**
You will count - **contaréis** (fam.), - **Ustedes contarán** (form.)
They will count - **contarán**

Past (Preterit)

SING. I counted *or* I did count - **conté**
You counted *or* you did count - **contaste** (fam.), - **Usted contó** (form.)
He/she/it counted *or* he/she/it did count - **contó**

PLUR. We counted *or* we did count - **contamos**
You counted *or* you did count - **contasteis** (fam.), - **Ustedes contaron** (form.)
They counted *or* they did count - **contaron**

Past (Indefinite)

SING. I have counted - **he contado**
You have counted - **has contado** (fam.), - **Usted ha contado** (form.)
He/she/it has counted - **ha contado**

PLUR. We have counted - **hemos contado**
You have counted - **habéis contado** (fam.), **Ustedes han contado** (form.)
They have counted - **han contado**

Past (Imperfect *or* Continuous)

SING. I was counting *or* I used to count - **contaba**
You were counting *or* you used to count - **contabas** (fam.), - **Usted contaba** (form.)
He/she/it was counting *or* he/she/it used to count - **contaba**

PLUR. We were counting *or* we used to count - **contábamos**
You were counting *or* you used to count - **contabais** (fam.), - **Ustedes contaban** (form.)
They were counting *or* they used to count - **contaban**

Gerund

Counting *or* Relating - **contando**

To Decide - **Decidir**
(Deth-ee-dear)

Present

SING. I decide, I do decide *or* I am deciding - **decido**
You decide, you do decide *or* you are deciding - **decides** (fam.), - **Usted decide** (form.)
He/she/it decides, he/she/it does decide *or* he/she/it is deciding - **decide**

PLUR. We decide, we do decide *or* we are deciding - **decidimos**
You decide, you do decide *or* you are deciding - **decidís** (fam.), - **Ustedes deciden** (form.)
They decide, they do decide *or* they are deciding - **deciden**

Future

SING. I shall decide - **decidiré**
You will decide - **decidirás** (fam), - **Usted decidirá** (form.)
He/she/it will decide - **decidirá**

PLUR. We shall decide - **decidiremos**
You will decide - **decidiréis** (fam.), - **Ustedes decidirán** (form.)
They will decide - **decidirán**

Past (Preterit)

SING. I decided *or* I did decide - **decidí**
You decided *or* you did decide - **decidiste** (fam.), - **Usted decidió** (form.)
He/she/it decided *or* he/she/it did decide - **decidió**

PLUR. We decided *or* we did decide - **decidimos**
You decided *or* you did decide - **decidisteis** (fam.), - **Ustedes decidieron** (form.)
They decided *or* they did decide - **decidieron**

Past (Indefinite)

SING. I have decided - **he decidido**
You have decided - **has decidido** (fam.), - **Usted ha decidido** (form.)
He/she/it has decided - **ha decidido**

PLUR. We have decided - **hemos decidido**
You have decided - **habéis decidido** (fam.), - **Ustedes han decidido** (form.)
They have decided - **han decidido**

Past (Imperfect *or* Continuous)

SING. I was deciding *or* I used to decide - **decidía**
You were deciding *or* you used to decide - **decidías** (fam.), - **Usted decidía** (form.)
He/she/it was deciding *or* he/she/it used to decide - **decidía**

PLUR. We were deciding *or* we used to decide - **decidíamos**
You were deciding *or* you used to decide - **decidíais** (fam.), - **Ustedes decidían** (form.)
They were deciding *or* they used to decide - **decidían**

Gerund

Deciding - **decidiendo**

To Do - **Hacer**
(Hath - air)
(Also to make)

Present

SING I do, I do do *or* I am doing - **yo hago**
You do, you do do *or* you are doing - **tú haces** (fam), - **Usted hace** (form)
He/she/it does, he/she/it does do *or* he/she/it is doing - **hace**

PLUR We do, we do do *or* we are doing - **hacemos**
You do, you do do *or* you are doing - **hacéis** (fam), - **Ustedes hacen** (form)
They do, they do do *or* they are doing - **hacen**

Future

SING.I shall do - **haré**
You will do - **harás** (fam), - **Usted hará** (form)
He/she/it will do - **hará**

PLUR We shall do - **haremos**
You will do - **haréis** (fam), - **Ustedes harán** (form)
They will do - **harán**

Past (Preterit)

SING I did *or* did do - **hice**
You did *or* you did do - **hiciste** (fam), - **Usted hizo** (form)
He/she/it did *or* he/she/it did do - **hizo**

PLUR. We did *or* we did do - **hicimos**
You did *or* you did do - **hicisteis** (fam), - **Ustedes hicieron** (form)
They did *or* they did do - **hicieron**

Past (Indefinite)

SING. I have done - **he hecho**
You have done - **has hecho** (fam), - **Usted ha hecho** (form)
He/she/it has done - **ha hecho**

PLUR. We have done - **hemos hecho**
You have done - **habéis hecho** (fam), - **Ustedes han hecho** (form)
They have done - **han hecho**

Past (Imperfect *or* Continuous)

SING. I was doing *or* I used to do - **hacía**
You were doing *or* you used to do - **hacías** (fam), - **Usted hacía** (form)
He/she/it was doing *or* he/she/it used to do - **hacía**

PLUR. We were doing *or* we used to do - **hacíamos**
You were doing *or* you used to do - **hacíais** (fam), - **Ustedes hacían** (form)
They were doing *or* they used to do - **hacían**

Gerund

Doing *or* making - **haciendo**

To Drink - **Beber**
(Beb-air)

Present

SING. I drink, I do drink *or* I am drinking - **yo bebo**
You drink, you do drink *or* you are drinking - **tú bebes** (fam.), - **Usted bebe** (form.)
He/she/it drinks, he/she/it does drink *or* he/she/it is drinking - **bebe**

PLUR. We drink, we do drink *or* we are drinking - **bebemos**
You drink, you do drink *or* you are drinking - **bebéis** (fam.), - **Ustedes beben** (form.)
They drink, they do drink *or* they are drinking - **beben**

Future

SING. I shall drink - **beberé**
You will drink - **beberás** (fam.), - **Usted beberá** (form.)
He/she/it will drink - **beberá**

PLUR. We shall drink - **beberemos**
You will drink - **beberéis** (fam.), - **Ustedes beberán** (form.)
They will drink - **beberán**

Past (Preterit)

SING. I drank *or* I did drink - **bebí**
You drank *or* you did drink - **bebiste** (fam.), - **Usted bebió** (form.)
He/she/it drank *or* he/she/it did drink - **bebió**

PLUR. We drank *or* we did drink - **bebimos**
You drank *or* you did drink - **bebisteis** (fam.), - **Ustedes bebieron** (form.)
They drank *or* they did drink - **bebieron**

Past (Indefinite)

SING. I have drunk - **he bebido**
You have drunk - **has bebido** (fam.), - **Usted ha bebido** (form.)
He/she/it has drunk - **ha bebido**

PLUR. We have drunk - **hemos bebido**
You have drunk - **habéis bebido** (fam.), - **Ustedes han bebido** (form.)
They have drunk - **han bebido**

Past (Imperfect *or* Continuous)

SING. I was drinking *or* I used to drink - **bebía**
You were drinking *or* you used to drink - **bebías** (fam.), - **Usted bebía** (form.)
He/she/it was drinking *or* he/she/it used to drink - **bebía**

PLUR. We were drinking *or* we used to drink - **bebíamos**
You were drinking *or* you used to drink - **bebíais** (fam), - **Ustedes bebían** (form)
They were drinking *or* they used to drink - **bebían**

Gerund

Drinking - **bebiendo**

To Drive (a car) - **Conducir**
(Con-doo-theer)
(Also to Conduct)

Present

SING. I drive, I do drive *or* I am driving - **conduzco**
You drive, you do drive *or* you are driving - **conduces** (fam.), - **Usted conduce** (form.)
He/she/it drives, he/she/it does drive *or* he/she/it is driving - **conduce**

PLUR. We drive, we do drive *or* we are driving - **conducimos**
You drive, you do drive *or* you are driving - **conducís** (fam.), - **Ustedes conducen** (form.)
They drive, they do drive *or* they are driving - **conducen**

Future

SING. I shall drive - **conduciré**
You will drive - **conducirás** (fam.), - **Usted conducirá** (form.)
He/she/it will drive - **conducirá**

PLUR. We shall drive - **conduciremos**
You will drive - **conduciréis** (fam.), - **Ustedes conducirán** (form.)
They will drive - **conducirán**

Past (Preterit)

SING. I drove *or* I did drive - **conduje**
You drove *or* you did drive - **condujiste** (fam.), - **Usted condujo** (form.)
He/she/it drove *or* he/she/it did drive - **condujo**

PLUR. We drove *or* we did drive - **condujimos**
You drove *or* you did drive - **condujisteis** (fam.), - **Ustedes condujeron** (form.)
They drove *or* they did drive - **condujeron**

Past (Indefinite)

SING. I have driven - **he conducido**
You have driven - **has conducido** (fam.), - **Usted ha conducido** (form.)
He/she/it has driven - **ha conducido**

PLUR. We have driven - **hemos conducido**
You have driven - **habéis conducido** (fam), - **Ustedes han conducido** (form.)
They have driven - **han conducido**

Past (Imperfect *or* Continuous)

SING. I was driving *or* I used to drive - **conducía**
You were driving *or* you used to drive - **conducías** (fam.), - **Usted conducía** (form.)
He/she/it was driving *or* he/she/it used to drive - **conducía**

PLUR. We were driving *or* we used to drive - **conducíamos**
You were driving *or* you used to drive - **conducíais** (fam.), - **Ustedes conducían** (form)
They were driving *or* they used to drive - **conducían**

Gerund

Driving - **conduciendo**

To Eat - **Comer**
(Com-air)

Present

SING. I eat, I do eat *or* I am eating - **yo como**
You eat, you do eat *or* you are eating - **tú comes** (fam.), - **Usted come** (form.)
He/she/it eats, he/she/it does eat *or* he/she/it is eating - **come**

PLUR. We eat, we do eat *or* we are eating - **comemos**
You eat, you do eat *or* you are eating - **coméis** (fam.), - **Ustedes comen** (form.)
They eat, they do eat *or* they are eating - **comen**

Future

SING. I shall eat - **comeré**
You will eat - **comerás** (fam.), - **Usted comerá** (form.)
He/she/it will eat - **comerá**

PLUR. We shall eat - **comeremos**
You will eat - **comeréis** (fam.), - **Ustedes comerán** (form.)
They will eat - **comerán**

Past (Preterit)

SING. I ate *or* I did eat - **comí**
You ate *or* you did eat - **comiste** (fam.), - **Usted comió** (form.)
He/she/it ate *or* he/she/it did eat - **comió**

PLUR. We ate *or* we did eat - **comimos**
You ate *or* you did eat - **comisteis** (fam.), - **Ustedes comieron** (form.)
They ate *or* they did eat - **comieron**

Past (Indefinite)

SING. I have eaten - **he comido**
You have eaten - **has comido** (fam.), - **Usted ha comido** (form.)
He/she/it has eaten - **ha comido**

PLUR. We have eaten - **hemos comido**
You have eaten - **hebéis comido** (fam.), - **Ustedes han comido** (form.)
They have eaten - **han comido**

Past (Imperfect or Continuous)

SING. I was eating *or* I used to eat - **comía**
You were eating *or* you used to eat - **comías** (fam.), - **Usted comía** (form.)
He/she/it was eating *or* he/she/it used to eat - **comía**

PLUR. We were eating *or* we used to eat - **comíamos**
You were eating *or* you used to eat - **comíais** (fam.), - **Ustedes comían** (form)
They were eating *or* they used to eat - **comían**

Gerund

Eating - **comiendo**

To Enjoy - **Gozar**
(Go-thaar)

Present

SING. I enjoy, I do enjoy *or* I am enjoying - **gozo**
You enjoy, you do enjoy *or* you are enjoying - **gozas** (fam.), - **Usted goza** (form.)
He/she/it enjoys, he/she/it does enjoy *or* he/she/it is enjoying - **goza**

PLUR. We enjoy, we do enjoy *or* we are enjoying - **gozamos**
You enjoy, you do enjoy *or* you are enjoying - **gozáis** (fam.), - **Ustedes gozan** (form.)
They enjoy, they do enjoy *or* they are enjoying - **gozan**

Future

SING. I shall enjoy - **gozaré**
You will enjoy - **gozarás** (fam.), - **Usted gozará** (form.)
He/she/it will enjoy - **gozará**

PLUR. We shall enjoy - **gozaremos**
You will enjoy - **gozaréis** (fam.), - **Ustedes gozarán** (form.)
They will enjoy - **gozarán**

Past (Preterit)

SING. I enjoyed *or* I did enjoy - **gocé**
You enjoyed *or* you did enjoy - **gozaste**, (fam.), - **Usted gozó** (form.)
He/she/it enjoyed *or* he/she/it did enjoy - **gozó**

PLUR. We enjoyed *or* we did enjoy - **gozamos**
You enjoyed *or* you did enjoy - **gozasteis** (fam.), - **Ustedes gozaron** (form.)
They enjoyed *or* they did enjoy - **gozaron**

Past (Indefinite)

SING. I have enjoyed - **he gozado**
You have enjoyed - **has gozado** (fam.), - **Usted ha gozado** (form.)
He/she/it has enjoyed - **ha gozado**

PLUR. We have enjoyed - **hemos gozado**
You have enjoyed - **habéis gozado** (fam.), - **Ustedes han gozado** (form.)
They have enjoyed - **han gozado**

Past (Imperfect or Continuous)

SING. I was enjoying *or* I used to enjoy - **gozaba**
You were enjoying *or* you used to enjoy - **gozabas** (fam.), - **Usted gozaba** (form.)
He/she/it was enjoying *or* he/she/it used to enjoy - **gozaba**

PLUR. We were enjoying *or* we used to enjoy - **gozábamos**
You were enjoying *or* you used to enjoy **gozabais** (fam.), - **Ustedes gozaban** (form.)
They were enjoying *or* they used to enjoy - **gozaban**

Gerund

Enjoying - **gozando**

To Enter - **Entrar**

Present

SING. I enter, I do enter *or* I am entering - **entro**
You enter, you do enter *or* you are entering - **entras** (fam.), - **Usted entra** (form.)
He/she/it enters, he/she/it does enter *or* he/she/it is entering - **entra**

PLUR. We enter, we do enter *or* we are entering - **entramos**
You enter, you do enter *or* you are entering - **entráis** (fam.), - **Ustedes entran** (form.)
They enter, they do enter *or* they are entering - **entran**

Future

SING. I shall enter - **entraré**
You will enter - **entrarás** (fam.), - **Usted entrará** (form.)
He/she/it will enter - **entrará**

PLUR. We shall enter - **entraremos**
You will enter - **entraréis** (fam.), - **Ustedes entrarán** (form.)
They will enter - **entrarán**

Past (Preterit)

SING. I entered *or* I did enter - **entré**
You entered *or* you did enter - **entraste** (fam.), - **Usted entró** (form.)
He/she/it entered *or* he/she/it did enter - **entró**

PLUR. We entered *or* we did enter - **entramos**
You entered *or* you did enter - **entrasteis** (fam.), - **Ustedes entraron** (form.)
They entered *or* they did enter - **entraron**

Past (Indefinite)

SING. I have entered - **he entrado**
You have entered - **has entrado** (fam.), - **Usted ha entrado** (form.)
He/she/it has entered - **ha entrado**

PLUR. We have entered - **hemos entrado**
You have entered - **habéis entrado** (fam.), - **Ustedes han entrado** (form.)
They have entered - **han entrado**

Past (Imperfect or Continuous)

SING. I was entering *or* I used to enter - **entraba**
You were entering *or* you used to enter - **entrabas** (fam.), - **Usted entraba** (form.)
He/she/it was entering *or* he/she/it used to enter - **entraba**

PLUR. We were entering *or* we used to enter - **entrábamos**
You were entering *or* you used to enter - **entrabais** (fam.), - **Ustedes entraban** (form.)
They were entering *or* they used to enter - **entraban**

Gerund

Entering - **entrando**

To Fall - **Caer**
(Kai-air)

Present

SING. I fall, I do fall *or* I am falling - **caigo**
You fall, you do fall *or* you are falling - **tú caes** (fam.), - **Usted cae** (form.)
He/she/it falls, he/she/it does fall *or* he/she/it is falling - **cae**

PLUR. We fall, we do fall *or* we are falling - **caemos**
You fall, you do fall *or* you are falling - **caéis** (fam.), - **Ustedes caen** (form.)
They fall, they do fall *or* they are falling - **caen**

Future

SING. I shall fall - **caeré**
You will fall - **caerás** (fam.), - **Usted caerá** (form.)
He/she/it will fall - **caerá**

PLUR. We shall fall - **caeremos**
You will fall - **caeréis** (fam.), - **Ustedes caerán** (form.)
They will fall - **caerán**

Past (Preterit)

SING. I fell *or* I did fall - **caí**
You fell *or* you did fall - **caíste** (fam.), - **Usted cayó** (form.)
He/she/it fell *or* he/she/it did fall - **cayó**

PLUR. We fell *or* we did fall - **caímos**
You fell *or* you did fall - **caísteis** (fam.), - **Ustedes cayeron** (form.)
They fell *or* they did fall - **cayeron**

Past (Indefinite)

SING. I have fallen - **he caído**
You have fallen - **has caído** (fam.), - **Usted ha caído** (form.)
He/she/it has fallen - **ha caído**

PLUR. We have fallen - **hemos caído**
You have fallen - **habéis caído** (fam), - **Ustedes han caído** (form.)
They have fallen - **han caído**

Past (Imperfect or Continuous)

SING. I was falling *or* I used to fall - **caía**
You were falling *or* you used to fall - **caías** (fam.), - **Usted caía** (form.)
He/she/it was falling *or* he/she/it used to fall - **caía**

PLUR. We were falling *or* we used to fall - **caíamos**
You were falling *or* you used to fall - **caíais** (fam.), - **Ustedes caían** (form.)
They were falling *or* they used to fall - **caían**

Gerund

Falling - **cayendo**

To Feel - **Sentir**
(*Sent-ear*)
(Also to Regret)

Present

SING. I feel, I do feel *or* I am feeling - **siento**
You feel, you do feel *or* you are feeling - **sientes** (fam.). - **Usted siente** (form.)
He/she/it feels, he/she/it does feel *or* he/she/it is feeling - **siente**

PLUR. We feel, we do feel *or* we are feeling - **sentimos**
You feel, you do feel *or* you are feeling - **sentís** (fam.), - **Ustedes sienten** (form.)
They feel, they do feel *or* they are feeling - **sienten**

Future

SING. I shall feel - **sentiré**
You will feel - **sentirás** (fam.), - **Usted sentirá** (form.)
He/she/it will feel - **sentirá**

PLUR. We shall feel - **sentiremos**
You will feel - **sentiréis** (fam.), - **Ustedes sentirán** (form.)
They will feel - **sentirán**

Past (Preterit)

SING. I felt *or* I did feel - **sentí**
You felt *or* you did feel - **sentiste** (fam.), - **Usted sintió** (form.)
He/she/it felt *or* he/she/it did feel - **sintió**

PLUR. We felt *or* we did feel - **sentimos**
You felt *or* you did feel - **sentisteis** (fam.), - **Ustedes sintieron** (form.)
They felt *or* they did feel - **sintieron**

Past (Indefinite)

SING. I have felt - **he sentido**
You have felt - **has sentido** (fam.), - **Usted ha sentido** (form.)
He/she/it has felt - **ha sentido**

PLUR. We have felt - **hemos sentido**
You have felt - **habéis sentido** (fam.), - **Ustedes han sentido** (form.)
They have felt - **han sentido**

Past (Imperfect or Continuous)

SING. I was feeling *or* I used to feel - **sentía**
You were feeling *or* you used to feel - **sentías** (fam.), - **Usted sentía** (form.)
He/she/it was feeling *or* he/she/it used to feel - **sentía**

PLUR. We were feeling *or* we used to feel - **sentíamos**
You were feeling *or* you used to feel - **sentíais** (fam.), - **Ustedes sentían** (form.)
They were feeling *or* they used to feel - **sentían**

Gerund

Feeling *or* regretting - **sintiendo**

To Find - **Encontrar**

Present

SING. I find, I do find *or* I am finding - **encuentro**
You find, you do find *or* you are finding - **encuentras** (fam.), - **Usted encuentra** (form.)
He/she/it finds, he/she/it does find *or* he/she/it is finding - **encuentra**

PLUR. We find, we do find *or* we are finding - **encontramos**
You find, you do find *or* you are finding - **encontráis** (fam.), - **Ustedes encuentran** (form.)
They find, they do find *or* they are finding - **encuentran**

Future

SING. I shall find - **encontraré**
You will find - **encontrarás** (fam.), - **Usted encontrará** (form.)
He/she/it will find - **encontrará**

PLUR. We shall find - **encontraremos**
You will find - **encontraréis** (fam.), - **Ustedes encontrarán** (form.)
They will find - **encontrarán**

Past (Preterit)

SING. I found *or* I did find - **encontré**
You found *or* you did find - **encontraste** (fam.), - **Usted encontró** (form.)
He/she/it found *or* he/she/it did find - **encontró**

PLUR. We found *or* we did find - **encontramos**
You found *or* you did find - **encontrasteis** (fam.), - **Ustedes encontraron** (form.)
They found *or* they did find - **encontraron**

Past (Indefinite)

SING. I have found - **he encontrado**
You have found - **has encontrado** (fam.), - **Usted ha encontrado** (form.)
He/she/it has found - **ha encontrado**

PLUR. We have found - **hemos encontrado**
You have found - **habéis encontrado** (fam.), - **Ustedes han encontrado** (form.)
They have found - **han encontrado**

Past (Imperfect or Continuous)

SING. I was finding *or* I used to find - **encontraba**
You were finding *or* you used to find - **encontrabas** (fam.), - **Usted encontraba** (form.)
He/she/it was finding *or* he/she/it used to find - **encontraba**

PLUR. We were finding *or* we used to find - **encontrábamos**
You were finding *or* you used to find - **encontrabais** (fam.), - **Ustedes encontraban** (form.)
They were finding *or* they used to find - **encontraban**

Gerund

Finding - **encontrando**

To Finish - **Terminar**

Present

SING. I finish, I do finish *or* I am finishing - **termino**
You finish, you do finish *or* you are finishing - **terminas** (fam.), - **Usted termina** form.)
He/she/it finishes, he/she/it does finish *or* he/she/it is finishing - **termina**

PLUR. We finish, we do finish *or* we are finishing - **terminamos**
You finish, you do finish *or* you are finishing - **termináis** (fam.), - **Ustedes terminan** (form.)
They finish, they do finish *or* they are finishing - **terminan**

Future

SING. I shall finish - **terminaré**
You will finish - **terminarás** (fam.), - **Usted terminará** (form.)
He/she/it will finish - **terminará**

PLUR. We shall finish - **terminaremos**
You will finish - **terminaréis** (fam.), - **Ustedes terminarán** (form.)
They will finish - **terminarán**

Past (Preterit)

SING. I finished *or* I did finish - **terminé**
You finished *or* you did finish - **terminaste** (fam.), - **Usted terminó** (form.)
He/she/it finished *or* he/she/it did finish - **terminó**

PLUR. We finished *or* we did finish - **terminamos**
You finished *or* you did finish - **terminasteis** (fam.), - **Ustedes terminaron** (form.)
They finished *or* they did finish - **terminaron**

Past (Indefinite)

SING. I have finished - **he terminado**
You have finished - **has terminado** (fam.), - **Usted ha terminado** (form.)
He/she/it has finished - **ha terminado**

PLUR. We have finished - **hemos terminado**
You have finished - **habéis terminado** (fam.), - **Ustedes han terminado** (form.)
They have finished - **han terminado**

Past (Imperfect or Continuous)

SING. I was finishing *or* I used to finish - **terminaba**
You were finishing *or* you used to finish - **terminabas** (fam.), - **Usted terminaba** (form.)
He/she/it was finishing *or* he/she/it used to finish - **terminaba**

PLUR. We were finishing *or* we used to finish - **terminábamos**
You were finishing *or* you used to finish - **terminabais** (fam.), - **Ustedes terminaban** (form.)
They were finishing *or* they used to finish - **terminaban**

Gerund

Finishing - **terminando**

To Fly - **Volar**

Present

SING. I fly, I do fly *or* I am flying - **vuelo**
You fly, you do fly *or* you are flying - **vuelas** (fam.), - **Usted vuela** (form.)
He/she/it flies, he/she/it does fly *or* he/she/it is flying - **vuela**

PLUR. We fly, we do fly *or* we are flying - **volamos**
You fly, you do fly *or* you are flying - **voláis** (fam.), - **Ustedes vuelan** (form.)
They fly, they do fly *or* they are flying - **vuelan**

Future

SING. I shall fly - **volaré**
You will fly - **volarás** (fam.), - **Usted volará** (form.)
He/she/it will fly - **volará**

PLUR. We shall fly - **volaremos**
You will fly - **volaréis** (fam.), - **Ustedes volarán** (form.)
They will fly - **volarán**

Past (Preterit)

SING. I flew *or* I did fly - **volé**
You flew *or* you did fly - **volaste** (fam.), - **Usted voló** (form.)
He/she/it flew *or* he/she/it did fly - **voló**

PLUR. We flew *or* we did fly - **volamos**
You flew *or* you did fly - **volasteis** (fam.), - **Ustedes volaron** (form.)
They flew *or* they did fly - **volaron**

Past (Indefinite)

SING. I have flown - **he volado**
You have flown - **has volado** (fam.), - **Usted ha volado** (form.)
He/she/it has flown - **ha volado**

PLUR. We have flown - **hemos volado**
You have flown - **habéis volado** (fam.), - **Ustedes han volado** (form.)
They have flow - **han volado**

Past (Imperfect or Continuous)

SING. I was flying *or* I used to fly - **volaba**
You were flying *or* you used to fly - **volabas** (fam.), - **Usted volaba** (form.)
He/she/it was flying *or* he/she/it used to fly - **volaba**

PLUR. We were flying *or* we used to fly - **volábamos**
You were flying *or* you used to fly - **volabais** (fam.), - **Ustedes volaban** (form.)
They were flying *or* they used to fly - **volaban**

Gerund

Flying - **volando**

To Forget - **Olvidar**

Present

SING. I forget, I do forget *or* I am forgetting - **olvido**
You forget, you do forget *or* you are forgetting - **olvidas** (fam.), - **Usted olvida** (form.)
He/she/it forgets, he/she/it does forget *or* he/she/it is forgetting - **olvida**

PLUR. We forget, we do forget *or* we are forgetting - **olvidamos**
You forget, you do forget *or* you are forgetting - **olvidáis** (fam.), - **Ustedes olvidan** (form.)
They forget, they do forget *or* they are forgetting - **olvidan**

Future

SING. I shall forget - **olvidaré**
You will forget - **olvidarás** (fam.), - **Usted olvidará** (form.)
He/she/it will forget - **olvidará**

PLUR. We shall forget - **olvidaremos**
You will forget - **olvidaréis** (fam.), - **Ustedes olvidarán** (form.)
They will forget - **olvidarán**

Past (Preterit)

SING. I forgot *or* I did forget - **olvidé**
You forgot *or* you did forget - **olvidaste** (fam.), - **Usted olvidó** (form.)
He/she/it forgot *or* he/she/it did forget - **olvidó**

PLUR. We forgot *or* we did forget - **olvidamos**
You forgot *or* you did forget - **olvidasteis** (fam.), - **Ustedes olvidaron** (form.)
They forgot *or* they did forget - **olvidaron**

Past (Indefinite)

SING. I have forgotten - **he olvidado**
You have forgotten - **has olvidado** (fam.), - **Usted ha olvidado** (form.)
He/she/it has forgotten - **ha olvidado**

PLUR. We have forgotten - **hemos olvidado**
You have forgotten - **habéis olvidado** (fam.), - **Ustedes han olvidado** (form.)
They have forgotten - **han olvidado**

Past (Imperfect or Continuous)

SING. I was forgetting *or* I used to forget - **olvidaba**
You were forgetting *or* you used to forget - **olvidabas** (fam.), - **Usted olvidaba** (form.)
He/she/it was forgetting *or* he/she/it used to forget - **olvidaba**

PLUR. We were forgetting *or* we used to forget - **olvidábamos**
You were forgetting *or* you used to forget - **olvidabais** (fam.), - **Ustedes olvidaban** (form.)
They were forgetting *or* they used to forget - **olvidaban**

Gerund

Forgetting - **olvidando**

To Get - **Conseguir**

(Con-seg-ear)

Also To Obtain or Attain

(Not to be confused with To Become - **Ponerse**, as to become sick)

Present

SING. I get, I do get *or* I am getting - **yo consigo**
You get, you do get *or* you are getting - **tú consigues** (fam.), - **Usted consigue** (form.)
He/she/it gets, he/she/it does get *or* he/she/it is getting - **consigue**

PLUR. We get, we do get *or* we are getting **conseguimos**
You get, you do get *or* you are getting **conseguís** (fam.), **Ustedes consiguen** (form.)
They get, they do get *or* they are getting **consiguen**

Future

SING. I shall get - **conseguiré**
You will get - **conseguirás** (fam.), - **Usted conseguirá** (form.)
He/she/it will get - **conseguirá**

PLUR. We shall get - **conseguiremos**
You will get - **conseguiréis** (fam.), **Ustedes conseguirán** (form.)
They will get - **conseguirán**

Past (Preterit)

SING. I got *or* I did get **consiguí**
You got *or* you did get - **conseguiste** (fam.), - **Usted consiguió** (form.)
He/she/it got *or* he/she/it did get - **consiguió**

PLUR. We got *or* we did get - **conseguimos**
You got *or* you did get - **conseguisteis** (fam.), - **Ustedes consiguieron** (form.)
They got *or* they did get - **consiguieron**

Past (Indefinite)

SING. I have got - **he conseguido**
You have got - **has conseguido** (fam.), - **Usted ha conseguido** (form.)
He/she/it has got - **ha conseguido**

PLUR. We have got - **hemos conseguido**
You have got - **habéis conseguido** (fam.), - **Ustedes han conseguido** (form.)
They have got - **han conseguido**

Past (Imperfect or Continuous)

SING. I was getting *or* I used to get - **conseguía**
You were getting *or* you used to get - **conseguías** (fam.), - **Usted conseguía** (form.)
He/she/it was getting *or* he/she/it used to get - **conseguía**

PLUR. We were getting *or* we used to get - **conseguíamos**
You were getting *or* you used to get - **conseguíais** (fam.), - **Ustedes conseguían** (form.).
They were getting *or* they used to get - **conseguían**

Gerund

Getting, Attaining *or* Obtaining - **consiguiendo**

To Give - **Dar**

Present

SING.I give, I do give *or* I am giving - **yo doy**
You give, you do give *or* you are giving - **tú das,** (fam.), - **Usted da** (form)
He /she/it gives, he/she/it does give *or* he/she/it is giving - **da**

PLUR.We give, we do give. *or* we are giving - **damos**
You give, you do give *or* you are giving - **dais**(fam.), - **Ustedes dan** (form)
He/she/it gives, he/she/it does give *or* he/she/it is giving - **dan**

Future

SING. I shall give - **daré**
You will give -**darás,** (fam.), - **Usted dará** (form.)
He/she/it will give - **dará**

PLUR. We shall give - **daremos**
You will give -**daréis** (fam.) - **Ustedes darán** (form.)
They will give - **darán**

Past (Preterit)

SING.I gave *or* I did give - **di**
You gave *or* you did give - **diste** (fam.), - **Usted dio** (form.)
He/she/it gave *or* he/she/it did give - **dio**

PLUR.We gave *or* we did give - **dimos**
You gave *or* you did give - **disteis** (fam.), - **Ustedes dieron** (form.)
They gave *or* they did give - **dieron**

Past (Indefinite)

SING.I have given - **he dado**
You have given - **has dado** (fam.), - **Usted ha dado** (form.)
He/she/it has given - **ha dado**

PLUR.We have given - **hemos dado**
You have given - **habéis dado** (fam.), - **Ustedes han dado** (form.)
They have given - **han dado**

Past (Imperfect *or* Continuous)

SING.I was giving *or* I used to give - **daba**
You were giving *or* you used to give - **dabas** (fam.), - **Usted daba** (form.)
He/she/it was giving *or* he/she/it used to give - **daba**

PLUR.We were giving *or* we used to give - **dábamos**
You were giving *or* you used to give - **dabais** (fam.)m - **Ustedes daban** (form.)
They were giving *or* they used to give - **daban**

Gerund

Giving - **dando**

To Go - **Ir**
(Ear)
(Not to be confused with to leave or depart - **marchar**, or to go out - **salir**)

Present

SING.I go, I do go *or* I am going - **voy**
You go, you do go *or* you are going - **vas** (fam.), - **Usted va** (form.)
He/she/it goes, he/she/it does go *or* he/she/it is going - **va**

PLUR.We go, we do go *or* we are going - **vamos**
You go, you do go *or* you are going - **vais** (fam.), - **Ustedes van** (form.)
They go, they do go *or* they are going - **van**

Future

SING.I shall go - **iré**
You will go -**irás** (fam.), - **Usted irá** (form.)
He/she/it will go - **irá**

PLUR.We shall go - **iremos**
You will go - **iréis** (fam.), - **Ustedes irán** (form.)
They will go - **irán**

Past (Preterit)

SING.I went *or* I did go - **fui**
You went *or* you did go - **fuiste** (fam.), - **Usted fue** (form.)
He/she/it went *or* he/she/it didi go - **fue**

PLUR.We went *or* we did go - **fuimos**
You went *or* you did go -**fuisteis** (fam.), - **Ustedes fueron** (form.)
They went *or* they did go - **fueron**

Past (Indefinite)

SING.I have gone *or* I have been - **he ido**
You have gone *or* you have been - **has ido** (fam.), - **Usted ha ido** (form.)
He/she/it has gone *or* he/she/it has been - **ha ido**

PLUR.We have gone *or* we have been - **hemos ido**
You have gone *or* you have been - **habéis ido** (fam.)m - **Ustedes han ido** (form.)
They have gone *or* they have been - **han ido**

Past (Imperfect *or* Continuous)

SING.I was going *or* I used to go - **iba**
You were going *or* you used to go - **ibas** (fam.), - **Usted iba** (form.)
He/she/it was going *or* he/she/it used to go - **iba**

PLUR.We were going *or* we used to go - **íbamos**
You were going *or* you used to go - **ibais** (fam.), - **Ustedes iban** (form.)
They were going *or* they used to go - **iban**

Gerund

Going -**yendo**

To Go On - **Seguir**
(Seg-ear)
(Also to follow *or* continue)

Present

SING. I go on, I do go on *or* I am going on - **sigo**
You go on, you do go on *or* you are going on - **sigues** (fam.), - **Usted sigue** (form.)
He/she/it goes on, he/she/it does go on *or* he/she/it is going on - **sigue**

PLUR. We go on, we do go on *or* we are going on - **seguimos**
You go on, you do go on *or* you are going on - **seguís** (fam.), - **Ustedes siguen** (form.)
They go on, they do go on *or* they are going on - **siguen**

Future

SING. I shall go on - **seguiré**
You will go on - **seguirás** (fam.), - **Usted seguirá** (form.)
He/she/it will go on - **seguirá**

PLUR. We shall go on - **seguiremos**
You will go on - **seguiréis** (fam.), - **Ustedes seguirán** (form.)
They will go on - **seguirán**

Past (Preterit)

SING. I went on *or* I did go on - **seguí**
You went on *or* you did go on - **seguiste** (fam.), - **Usted siguió** (form.)
He/she/it went on *or* he/she/it did go on - **siguió**

PLUR. We went on *or* we did go on - **seguimos**
You went on *or* you did go on - **seguisteis** (fam.), - **Ustedes siguieron** (form.)
They went on *or* they did go on - **siguieron**

Past (Indefinite)

SING. I have gone on - **he seguido**
You have gone on - **has seguido** (fam.), - **Usted ha seguido** (form.)
He/she/it has gone one - **ha seguido**

PLUR. We have gone on - **hemos seguido**
You have gone on - **habéis seguido** (fam.), - **Ustedes han seguido** (form.)
They have gone on - **han seguido**

Past (Imperfect *or* Continuous)

SING. I was going on *or* I used to go on - **seguía**
You were going on *or* you used to go on - **seguías** (fam.), - **Usted seguía** (form.)
He/she/it was going on *or* he/she/it used to go on - **seguía**

PLUR. We were going on *or* we used to go on - **seguíamos**
You were going on *or* you used to go on - **seguíais** (fam.), - **Ustedes seguían** (form.)
They were going on *or* they used to go on - **seguían**

Gerund

Going on, Following *or* Continuing - **siguiendo**

To Go Out - **Salir**
(Sal-ear)

Present

SING.I go out, I do go out *or* I am going out - **salgo**
You go out, you do go out *or* you are going out - **sales** (fam.), - **Usted sale** (form.)
He/she/it goes out, *or* he/she/it does go out *or* he/she/it is going out - **sale**

PLUR.We go out, we do go out *or* we are going out - **salimos**
You go out, you do go out *or* you are going out - **salis** (fam.), - **Ustedes salen** (form.)
They go out, they do go out *or* they are going out - **salen**

Future

SING.I shall go out - **saldré**
You will go out - **saldrás** (fam.), - **Usted saldrá** (form.)
He/she/it will go out - **saldrá**

PLUR.We shall go out - **saldremos**
You will go out - **saldréis** (fam.), - **Ustedes saldrán** (form.)
They will go out - **saldrán**

Past (Preterit)

SING.I went out *or* I did go out - **sali**
You went out *or* you did go out - **saliste** (fam.), - **Usted salió** (form.)
He/she/it went out *or* he/she/it did go out - **salio**

PLUR.We went out *or* we did go out - **salimos**
You went out *or* you did go out - **salisteis** (fam.), - **Ustedes salieron** (form.)
They went out *or* they did go out - **salieron**

Past (Indefinite)

SING.I have been out - **he salido**
You have been out - **has salido** (fam.), - **Usted ha salido** (form.)
He/she/it has been out - **ha salido**

PLUR.We have been out - **hemos salido**
You have been out - **habéis salido** (fam.), - **Ustedes han salido** (form.)
They have been out - **han salido**

Past (Imperfect *or* Continuous)

SING.I was going out *or* I used to go out - **salia**
You were going out *or* you used to go out - **saliás** (fam.), - **Usted salia** (form.)
He/she/it was going out *or* he/she/it used to go out - **salia**

PLUR.We were going out *or* we used to go out - **saliamos**
You were going out *or* you used to go out - **saliais** (fam.), - **Ustedes salian** (form.)
They were going out *or* they used to go out - **salian**

Gerund

Going out - **saliendo**

To Happen - **Suceder**
(Soo-thay-dair)

Present
SING.It happens, it does happen *or* it is happening - **sucede**

PLUR. - **suceden**

Future
SING.It will happen - **sucedeŕa**

PLUR. - **sucederán**

Past (Preterit)
SING.It happened *or* it did happen - **sucedió**

PLUR. - **sucedieron**

Past (Indefinite)
SING.It has happened - **ha sucedido**

PLUR. - **han sucedido**

Past (Imperfect *or* Continuous)
SING.It was happening *or* it used to happen - **sucedia**

PLUR. - **sucedian**

Gerund
Happening - **sucediendo**

To Have - **Tener**
(Ten-air)
(Also to Hold)

Present

SING.I have, I do have *or* I am having - **yo tengo**
You have, you do have *or* you are having - **tú tienes** (fam.), - **Usted tiene** (form.)
He/she/it has, he/she/it does have *or* he/she/it is having - **tiene**

PLUR.We have, we do have *or* we are having - **tenemos**
You have, you do have *or* you are having - **tenéis** (fam.), - **Ustedes tienen** (form.)
They have, they do have *or* they are having - **tienen**

Future

SING.I shall have - **tendré**
You will have - **tendrás** (fam.), - **Usted tendrá** (form.)
He/she/it will have - **tendra**

PLUR.We shall have - **tendremos**
You will have - **tendréis** (fam.), - **Ustedes tendrán** (form.)
They will have - **tendrán**

Past (Preterit)

SING.I had *or* I did have - **tuve**
You had *or* you did have - **tuviste** (fam.), - **Usted tuvo** (form.)
He/she/it had *or* he/she/it did have - **tuvo**

PLUR.We had *or* we did have - **tuvimos**
You had *or* you did have - **tuvisteis** (fam.), - **Ustedes tuvieron** (form.)
They had *or* they did have - **tuvieron**

Past (Indefinite)

SING.I have had - **he tenido**
You have had - **has tenido** (fam.), - **Usted ha tenido** (form.)
He/she/it has had - **ha tenido**

PLUR.We have had - **hemos tenido**
You have had - **habéis tenido** (fam.), - **Ustedes han tenido** (form.)
They have had - **han tenido**

Past (Imperfect *or* Continuous)

SING.I was having *or* I used to have - **tenia**
You were having *or* you used to have - **tenías** (fam.), - **Usted tenia** (form.)
He/she/it was having *or* he/she/it used to have - **tenía**

PLUR.We were having *or* we used to have - **teníamos**
You were having *or* you used to have - **teníais** (fam.), - **Ustedes tenian** (form).
They were having *or* they used to have - **tenían**

Gerund

Having - **teniendo**

To Have To (Must) - **Tener que**
(Ten-air kay)

Present

SING.I have to, I do have to *or* I am having to - **tengo que**
You have to, you do have to *or* you are having to - **tienes que** (fam.), - **Usted tiene que** (form.)
He/she/it has to, he/she/it does have to *or* he/she/it is having to - **tiene que**

PLUR.We have to, we do have to *or* we are having to - **tenemos que**
You have to, you do have to *or* you are having to - **tenéis que** (fam.), - **Ustedes tienen que** (form.)
They have to, they do have to *or* they are having to - **tienen que**

Future

SING.I shall have to - **tendré que**
You will have to - **tendrás que** (fam.), - **Usted tendrá que** (form.)
He/she/it will have to - **tendrá que**

PLUR.We shall have to - **tendremos que**
You will have to - **tendréis que** (fam.), - **Ustedes tendrán que** (form.)
They will have to - **tendrán que**

Past (Preterit)

SING.I had to *or* I did have to - **tuve que**
You had to *or* you did have to - **tuviste que** (fam.), - **Usted tuvo que** (form.)
He/she/it had to *or* he/she/it did have to - **tuvo que**

PLUR.We had to *or* we did have to - **tuvimos que**
You had to *or* you did have to - **tuvisteis que** (fam.), - **Ustedes tuvieron que** (form.)
They had to *or* they did have to - **tuvieron que**

Past (Indefinite)

SING.I have had to - **he tenido que**
You have had to - **has tenido que** (fam.), - **Usted ha tenido que** (form.)
He/she/it has had to - **ha tenido que**

PLUR.We have had to - **hemos tenido que**
You have had to - **habéis tenido que** (fam.), - **Ustedes han tenido que** (form.)
They have had to - **han tenido que**

Past (Imperfect *or* Continuous)

SING.I was having to *or* I used to have to - **tenía que**
You were having to *or* you used to have to - **tenías que** (fam.), - **Usted tenía que** (form.)
He/she/it was having to *or* he/she/it used to have to -**tenía que**

PLUR.We were having to *or* we used to have to - **teníamos que**
You were having to *or* you used to have to - **teníais que** (fam.), - **Ustedes tenían que** (form.)
They were having to *or* they used to have to - **tenían que**

Gerund

Having to - **teniendo que**

To Hear - **Oír**
(*Oy-ear*)

Present

SING. I hear, I do hear *or* I am hearing - **oigo**
You hear, you do hear *or* you are hearing - **oyes** (fam.), - **Usted oye** (form.)
He/she/it hears, he/she/it does hear *or* he/she/it is hearing - **oye**

PLUR. We hear, we do hear *or* we are hearing - **oímos**
You hear, you do hear *or* you are hearing - **oís** (fam.), - **Ustedes oyen** (form.)
They hear, they do hear *or* they are hearing - **oyen**

Future

SING. I shall hear - **oiré**
You will hear - **oirás** (fam.), - **Usted oirá** (form.)
He/she/it will hear - **oirá**

PLUR. We shall hear - **oiremos**
You will hear - **oiréis** (fam.), - **Ustedes oirán** (form.)
They will hear - **oirán**

Past (Preterit)

SING. I heard *or* I did hear - **oí**
You heard *or* you did hear - **oíste** (fam.), - **Usted oyó** (form.)
He/she/it heard *or* he/she/it did hear - **oyó**

PLUR. We heard *or* we did hear - **oímos**
You heard *or* you did hear - **oísteis** (fam.), - **Ustedes oyeron** (form.)
They heard *or* they did hear - **oyeron**

Past (Indefinite)

SING. I have heard - **he oído**
You have heard - **has oído** (fam.), - **Usted ha oído** (form.)
He/she/it has heard - **ha oído**

PLUR. We have heard - **hemos oído**
You have heard - **habéis oído** (fam.), - **Ustedes han oído** (form.)
They have heard - **han oído**

Past (Imperfect *or* Continuous)

SING. I was hearing *or* I used to hear - **oía**
You were hearing *or* you used to hear - **oías** (fam.), - **Usted oía** (form.)
He/she/it was hearing *or* he/she/it used to hear - **oía**

PLUR. We were hearing *or* we used to hear - **oíamos**
You were hearing *or* you used to hear - **oíais** (fam.), - **Ustedes oían** (form.)
They were hearing *or* they used to hear - **oían**

Gerund

Hearing - **oyendo**

To Hit - **Golpear**
(Gol-pay-ar)

Present

SING. I hit, I do hit *or* I am hitting - **golpeo**
You hit, you do hit *or* you are hitting - **golpeas** (fam.), - **Usted golpea** (form.)
He/she/it hits, he/she/it does hit *or* he/she/it is hitting - **golpea**

PLUR. We hit, we do hit *or* we are hitting - **golpeamos**
You hit, you do hit *or* you are hitting - **golpeáis** (fam.), - **Ustedes golpean** (form.)
They hit, they do hit *or* they are hitting - **golpean**

Future

SING. I shall hit - **golpearé**
You will hit - **golpearás** (fam.), - **Usted golpeará** (form.)
He/she/it will hit - **golpeará**

PLUR. We shall hit - **golpearemos**
You will hit - **golpearéis** (fam.), - **Ustedes golpearán** (form.)
They will hit - **golpearán**

Past (Preterit)

SING. I hit *or* I did hit - **golpeé**
You hit *or* you did hit - **golpeaste** (fam.), - **Usted golpeó** (form.)
He/she/it hit *or* he/she/it did hit - **golpeó**

PLUR. We hit *or* we did hit - **golpeamos**
You hit *or* you did hit - **golpeasteis** (fam.), - **Ustedes golpearon** (form.)
They hit *or* they did hit - **golpearon**

Past (Indefinite)

SING. I have hit - **he golpeado**
You have hit - **has golpeado** (fam.), - **Usted ha golpeado** (form.)
He/she/it has hit - **ha golpeado**

PLUR. We have hit - **hemos golpeado**
You have hit - **habeis golpeado** (fam.), - **Ustedes han golpeado** (form.)
They have hit - **han golpeado**

Past (Imperfect *or* Continuous)

SING. I was hitting *or* I used to hit - **golpeaba**
You were hitting *or* you used to hit - **golpeabas** (fam.)m - **Usted golpeaba** (form.)
He/she/it was hitting *or* he/she/it used to hit - **golpeaba**

PLUR. We were hitting *or* we used to hit - **golpeábamos**
You were hitting *or* you used to hit - **golpeabais** fam.), - **Ustedes golpeaban** (form.)
They were hitting *or* they used to hit - **golpeaban**

Gerund

Hitting - **golpeando**

To Keep - **Retener**
(*Ret-en-air*)

Present

SING. I keep, I do keep *or* I am keeping - **retengo**
You keep, you do keep *or* you are keeping - **retienes** (fam.), - **Usted retiene** (form.)
He/she/it keeps, he/she/it does keep *or* he/she/it is keeping - **retiene**

PLUR. We keep, we do keep *or* we are keeping - **retenemos**
You keep, you do keep *or* you are keeping - **retenéis** (fam.), - **Ustedes retienen** (form.)
They keep, they do keep *or* they are keeping - **retienen**

Future

SING. I shall keep - **retendré**
You will keep - **retendrás** (fam.), - **Usted retendrá** (form.)
He/she/it will keep - **retendrá**

PLUR. We shall keep - **retendremos**
You will keep - **retendréis** (fam.), - **Ustedes retendrán** (form.)
They will keep - **retendrán**

Past (Preterit)

SING. I kept *or* I did keep - **retuve**
You kept *or* you did keep - **retuviste** (fam.), - **Usted retuvo** (form.)
He/she/it kepr *or* he/she/it did keep - **retuvo**

PLUR. We kept *or* we did keep - **retuvimos**
You kept *or* you did keep - **retuvisteis** (fam.), - **Ustedes retuvieron** (form.)
They kept *or* they did keep - **retuvieron**

Past (Indefinite)

SING. I have kept - **he retenido**
You have kept - **has retenido** (fam.), - **Usted ha retenido** (form.)
He/she/it has kept - **ha retenido**

PLUR. We have kept - **hemos retenido**
You have kept - **habéis retenido** (fam.), - **Ustedes han retenido** (form.)
They have kept - **han retenido**

Past (Imperfect *or* Continuous)

SING. I was keeping *or* I used to keep - **retenia**
You were keeping *or* you used to keep - **retenías** (fam.), - **Usted retenía** (form.)
He/she/it was keeping *or* he/she/it used to keep - **retenia**

PLUR. We were keeping *or* we used to keep - **reteníamos**
You were keeping *or* you used to keep - **reteníais** (fam.), - **Ustedes retenían** (form.)
They were keeping *or* they used to keep - **retenían**

Gerund

Keeping *or* Retaining - **reteniendo**

To Know - **Saber**

(Sab-air)

(To know how, not to be confused with to know a person/place - **Conocer**, to be acquainted with)

Present

SING. I know *or* I do know - **yo sé**
You know *or* you do know - **tú sabes** (fam.), - **Usted sabe** (form.)
He/she/it knows *or* he/she/it does know - **sabe**

PLUR. We know *or* we do know - **sabemos**
You know *or* you do know - **sabéis** (fam.), - **Ustedes saben** (form.)
They know *or* they do know - **saben**

Future

SING. I shall know - **sabré**
You will know - **sabrás** (fam.), - **Usted sabrá** (form.)
He/she/it will know - **sabrá**

PLUR. We shall know - **sabremos**
You will know - **sabréis** (fam.), - **Ustedes sabrán** (form.)
They will know - **sabrán**

Past (Preterit)

SING. I knew *or* I did know - **supe**
You knew *or* you did know - **supiste** (fam.), - **Usted supo** (form.)
He/she/it knew *or* he/she/it did know - **supo**

PLUR. We knew or we did know - **supimos**
You knew *or* you did know - **supisteis** (fam.), - **Ustedes supieron** (form.)
They knew *or* they did know - **supieron**

Past (Indefinite)

SING. I have known - **he sabido**
You have known - **has sabido** (fam.), - **Usted ha sabido** (form.)
He/she/it has known - **ha sabido**

PLUR. We have known - **hemos sabido**
You have known - **habéis sabido** (fam.), - **Ustedes han sabido** (form.)
They have known - **han sabido**

Past (Imperfect or Continuous)

SING. I used to know - **sabía**
You used to know - **sabías** (fam.), - **Usted sabía** (form.)
He/she/it used to know - **sabía**

PLUR. We used to know - **sabíamos**
You used to know - **sabíais** (fam.), - **Ustedes sabían** (form.)
They used to know - **sabían**

Gerund

Knowing - **sabiendo**

To Know - **Conocer**
(Con-o-thair)
(To be acquainted with. See also to know - **Saber)**

Present

SING. I know *or* I do know - **conozco**
You know *or* you do know - **conoces** (fam.), - **Usted conoce** (form.)
He/she/it knows *or* he/she/it does know - **conoce**

PLUR. We know *or* we do know - **conocemos**
You know *or* you do know - **conocéis** (fam.), - **Ustedes conocen** (form.)
They know *or* they do know - **conocen**

Future

SING. I shall know - **conoceré**
You will know - **conocerás** (fam.), - **Usted conocerá** (form.)
He/she/it will know - **conocerá**

PLUR. We shall know - **conoceremos**
You will know - **conoceréis** (fam.), - **Ustedes conocerán** (form.)
They will know - **conocerán**

Past (Preterit)

SING. I knew *or* I did know - **conocí**
You knew *or* you did know - **conociste** (fam.), - **Usted conoció** (form.)
He/she/it knew *or* he/she/it did know - **conoció**

PLUR. We knew *or* we did know - **conocimos**
You knew *or* you did know - **conocisteis** (fam.), - **Ustedes conocieron** (form.)
They knew *or* they did know - **conocieron**

Past (Indefinite)

SING. I have known - **he conocido**
You have known - **has conocido** (fam.), - **Usted ha conocido** (form.)
He/she/it has known - **ha conocido**

PLUR. We have known - **hemos conocido**
You have known - **habéis conocido** (fam.), - **Ustedes han conocido** (form.)
They have known - **han conocido**

Past (Imperfect *or* Continuous)

SING. I used to know - **conocia**
You used to know - **conocias** (fam.) - **Usted conocia** (form.)
He/she/it used to know - **conocia**

PLUR. We used to know - **conociamos**
You used to know - **conociais** (fam.), - **Ustedes conocian** (form.)
They used to know - **conocian**

Gerund

Knowing - **conociendo**

To Learn - **Aprender**
(Ap-rend-air)

Present

SING. I learn, I do learn *or* I am learning - **aprendo**
You learn, you do learn *or* you are learning - **aprendes** (fam.), - **Usted aprende** (form.)
He/she/it learns, he/she/it does learn *or* he/she/it is learning - **aprende**

PLUR. We learn, we do learn *or* we are learning - **aprendemos**
You learn, you do learn *or* you are learning - **aprendéis** (fam.), - **Ustedes aprenden** (form.)
They learn, they do learn *or* they are learning - **aprenden**

Future

SING. I shall learn - **aprenderé**
You will learn - **aprenderás** (fam.), - **Usted aprenderá** (form.)
He/she/it will learn - **aprenderá**

PLUR. We shall learn - **aprenderemos**
You will learn - **aprenderéis** (fam.), - **Ustedes aprenderan** (form.)
They will learn - **aprenderan**

Past (Preterit)

SING. I learnt *or* I did learn - **aprendí**
You learnt *or* you did learn - **aprendiste** (fam.), - **Usted aprendió** (form.)
He/she/it learnt *or* he/she/it did learn - **aprendió**

PLUR. We learnt *or* we did learn - **aprendimos**
You learnt *or* you did learn - **aprendisteis** (fam.), - **Ustedes aprendieron** (form.)
They learnt *or* they did learn - **aprendieron**

Past (Indefinite)

SING. I have learned - **he aprendido**
You have learned - **has aprendido** (fam.), - **Usted ha aprendido** (form.)
He/she/it has learned - **ha aprendido**

PLUR. We have learned - **hemos aprendido**
You have learned - **habéis aprendido** (fam.), - **Ustedes han aprendido** (form.)
They have learned - **han aprendido**

Past (Imperfect *or* Continuous)

SING. I was learning *or* I used to learn - **aprendía**
You were learning *or* you used to learn - **aprendías** (fam.), - **Usted aprendía** (form.)
He/she/it was learning *or* he/she/it used to learn - **aprendía**

PLUR. We were learning *or* we used to learn - **aprendíamos**
You were learning *or* you used to learn - **aprendíais** (fam.), - **Ustedes aprendían** (form.)
They were learning *or* they used to learn - **aprendían**

Gerund

Learning - **aprendiendo**

To Leave *or* To Go Away - **Marchar**
(Also for an engine or machine To Run)

Present

SING. I leave, I do leave *or* I am leaving - **yo marcho**
You leave, you do leave *or* you are leaving - **tú marchas** (fam.), - **Usted marcha** (form.)
He/she/it leaves, he/she/it does leave *or* he/she/it is leaving - **marcha**

PLUR. We leave, we do leave *or* we are leaving - **marchamos**
You leave, you do leave *or* you are leaving - **marcháis** (fam.), - **Ustedes marchan** (form.)
They leave, they do leave *or* they are leaving - **marchan**

Future

SING. I shall leave - **marcharé**
You will leave - **marcharás** (fam.), - **Usted marchará** (form.)
He/she/it will leave - **marchará**

PLUR. We shall leave - **marcharemos**
You will leave - **marcharéis** (fam.), - **Ustedes marcharán** (form.)
They will leave - **marcharán**

Past (Preterit)

SING. I left *or* I did leave - **marché**
You left *or* you did leave - **marchaste** (fam.), - **Usted marchó** (form.)
He/she/it left *or* he/she/it did leave - **marchó**

PLUR. We left *or* we did leave - **marchamos**
You left *or* you did leave - **marchasteis** (fam.), - **Ustedes marcharon** (form.)
They left *or* they did leave - **marcharon**

Past (Indefinite)

SING. I have gone - **he marchado**
You have gone - **has marchado** (fam.), - **Usted ha marchado** (form.)
He/she/it has gone - **ha marchado**

PLUR. We have gone - **hemos marchado**
You have gone - **habéis marchado** (fam.), - **Ustedes han marchado** (form.)
They have gone - **han marchado**

Past (Imperfect *or* Continuous)

SING. I was leaving *or* I used to leave - **marchaba**
You were leaving *or* you used to leave - **marchabas** (fam.), - **Usted marchaba** (form.)
He/she/it was leaving *or* he/she/it used to leave - **marchaba**

PLUR. We were leaving *or* we used to leave - **marchábamos**
You were leaving *or* you used to leave - **marchabais** (fam.), - **Ustedes marchaban** (form.)
They were leaving *or* they used to leave - **marchaban**

Gerund

Leaving (or an engine running) - **marchando**

To Leave Alone - **Dejar**
(*Deck-ar*)
(Or to Let Be)
(Also To Leave Something Somewhere)

Present

SING. I leave, I do leave *or* I am leaving - **dejo**
You leave, you do leave *or* you are leaving - **dejas** (fam.), - **Usted deja** (form.)
He/she/it leaves, he/she/it does leave *or* he/she/it is leaving - **deja**

PLUR. We leave, we do leave *or* we are leaving - **dejamos**
You leave, you do leave *or* you are leaving - **dejáis** (fam.), - **Ustedes dejan** (form.)
They leave, they do leave *or* they are leaving - **dejan**

Future

SING. I shall leave - **dejaré**
You will leave - **dejarás** (fam.), - **Usted dejará** (form.)
He/she/it will leave - **dejará**

PLUR. We shall leave - **dejaremos**
You will leave - **dejaréis** (fam.), - **Ustedes dejarán** (form.)
They will leave - **dejarán**

Past (Preterit)

SING. I left *or* I did leave - **dejé**
You left *or* you did leave - **dejaste** (fam.), - **Usted dejó** (form.)
He/she/it left *or* he/she/it did leave - **dejó**

PLUR. We left *or* we did leave - **dejamos**
You left *or* you did leave - **dejasteis** (fam.), - **Ustedes dejaron** (form.)
They left *or* they did leave - **dejaron**

Past (Indefinite)

SING. I have left - **he dejado**
You have left - **has dejado** (fam.), - **Usted ha dejado** (form.)
He/she/it has left - **ha dejado**

PLUR. We have left - **hemos dejado**
You have left - **habéis dejado** (fam.), - **Ustedes han dejado** (form.)
They have left - **han dejado**

Past (Imperfect *or* Continuous)

SING. I was leaving *or* I used to leave - **dejaba**
You were leaving *or* you used to leave - **dejabas** (fam.), - **Usted dejaba** (form.)
He/she/it was leaving *or* he/she/it used to leave - **dejaba**

PLUR. We were leaving *or* we used to leave - **dejábamos**
You were leaving *or* you used to leave - **dejabais** (fam.), - **Ustedes dejaban** (form.)
They were leaving *or* they used to leave - **dejaban**

Gerund

Leaving *or* Letting Be - **dejando**

To Like - **Gustar**
(*Goos-tar*)

This verb causes us some confusion because it does not actually mean "to like", it means "to be pleasing to". For example, in English we say "I like the wine", in Spanish **me gusta el vino,** which literally translated is "to me is pleasing the wine". Therefore the use of the verb is affected by the singular or plural of that which is pleasing, for example "I like the wines" - "**me gustan los vinos**".

Present	**Single Item**	**Plural**
SING. I like, I do like, I am liking	**me gusta**	**me gustan**
You like, you do like, you are liking	**te gusta** (fam.)	**te gustan** (fam.)
You like, you do like, you are liking	**le gusta a Usted** (form.)	**le gustan a Usted** (form.)
He likes, he does like, he is liking	**le gusta a él**	**le gustan a él**
She likes, she does like, she is liking	**le gusta a ella**	**le gustan a ella**
PLUR. We like, we do like, we are liking	**nos gusta**	**nos gustan**
You like, you do like, you are liking	**os gusta** (fam.)	**os gustan** (fam.)
You like, you do like, you are liking	**les gusta a Ustedes** (form.)	**les gustan a Ustedes** (form.)
They like (masculine or mixed company)	**les gusta a ellos**	**les gustan a ellos**
They like (feminine)	**les gusta a ellas**	**les gustan a ellas**

Future (For "would like" use **Querer** page 106)

SING. I shall like	**me gustará**	**me gustarán**
You will like	**te gustará** (fam.)	**te gustarán** (fam.)
You will like	**le gustará a Usted** (form.)	**le gustarán a Usted** (form.)
He will like	**le gustará a él**	**le gustarán a él**
She will like	**le gustará a ella**	**le gustarán a ella**
PLUR. We shall like	**nos gustará**	**nos gustarán**
You will like	**os gustará** (fam.)	**os gustarán** (fam.)
You will like	**les gustará a Ustedes** (form.)	**les gustarán a Ustedes** (form.)
They (masculine or mixed)	**les gustará a ellos**	**les gustarán a ellos**
They (feminine)	**les gustará a ellas**	**les gustarán a ellas**

Past (Preterit)

SING. I liked or I did like	**me gustó**	**me gustaron**
You liked or you did like	**te gustó** (fam.)	**te gustaron** (fam.)
You liked or you did like	**le gustó a Usted** (form.)	**le gustaron a Usted** (form.)
He liked or he did like	**le gustó a él**	**le gustaron a él**
She liked or she did like	**le gustó a ella**	**le gustaron a ella**
PLUR. We liked or we did like	**nos gustó**	**nos gustaron**
You liked or you did like	**os gustó** (fam.)	**os gustaron** (fam.)
You liked or you did like	**les gustó a Ustedes** (form.)	**les gustaron a Ustedes** (form.)
They (masculine or mixed)	**les gustó a ellos**	**les gustaron a ellos**
They (feminine)	**les gustó a ellas**	**les gustaron a ellas**

Past (Indefinite)

(For this tense I suggest the use of the verb To Enjoy - **Gozar** page 36)

Past (Imperfect)

SING. I used to like	**me gustaba**	**me gustaban**
You used to like	**te gustaba** (fam.)	**te gustaban** (fam.)
You used to like	**le gustaba a Usted** (form.)	**le gustaban a Usted** (form.)
He used to like	**le gustaba a él**	**le gustaban a él**
She used to like	**le gustaba a ella**	**le gustaban a ella**
PLUR. We used to like	**nos gustaba**	**nos gustaban**
You used to like	**os gustaba** (fam.)	**os gustaban** (fam.)
You used to like	**les gustaba a Ustedes** (form.)	**les gustaban a Ustedes** (form.)
They (masculine or mixed)	**les gustaba a ellos**	**les gustaban a ellos**
They (feminine)	**les gustaba a ellas**	**les gustaban a ellas**

Gerund

Liking or to be pleasing to - **gustando**

To Listen - **Escuchar**
(Es-koo-char)

Present

SING. I listen, I do listen *or* I am listening - **escucho**
You listen, you do listen *or* you are listening - **escuchas** (fam.), - **Usted escucha** (form.)
He/she/it listens, he/she/it does listen *or* he/she/it is listening - **escucha**

PLUR. We listen, we do listen *or* we are listening - **escuchamos**
You listen, you do listen *or* you are listening - **escucháis** (fam.), - **Ustedes escuchan** (form.)
They listen, they do listen *or* they are listening - **escuchan**

Future

SING. I shall listen - **escucharé**
You will listen - **escucharás** (fam.), - **Usted escuchará** (form.)
He/she/it will listen - **escuchará**

PLUR. We shall listen - **escucharemos**
You will listen - **escucharéis** (fam.), - **Ustedes escucharán** (form.)
They will listen - **escucharán**

Past (Preterit)

SING. I listened *or* I did listen - **escuché**
You listened *or* you did listen - **escuchaste** (fam.), - **Usted escuchó** (form.)
He/she/it listened *or* he/she/it did listen - **escuchó**

PLUR. We listened *or* we did listen - **escuchamos**
You listened *or* you did listen - **escuchastéis** (fam.), - **Ustedes escucharon** (form.)
They listened *or* they did listen - **escucharon**

Past (Indefinite)

SING. I have listened - **he escuchado**
You have listened - **has escuchado** (fam.), - **Usted ha escuchado** (form.)
He/she/it has listened - **ha escuchado**

PLUR. We have listened - **hemos escuchado**
You have listened - **habéis escuchado** (fam.), - **Ustedes han escuchado** (form.)
They have listened - **han escuchado**

Past (Imperfect *or* Continuous)

SING. I was listening *or* I used to listen - **escuchaba**
You were listening *or* you used to listen - **escuchabas** (fam.), - **Usted escuchaba** (form.)
He/she/it was listening *or* he/she/it used to listen - **escuchaba**

PLUR. We were listening *or* we used to listen - **escuchábamos**
You were listening *or* you used to listen - **escuchabais** (fam.), - **Ustedes escuchaban** (form.)
They were listening *or* they used to listen - **escuchaban**

Gerund

Listening - **escuchando**

To Live - **Vivir**
(Viv-ear)

Present

SING. I live, I do live *or* I am living - **yo vivo**
You live, you do live *or* you are living - **tú vives** (fam.), - **Usted vive** (form.)
He/she/it lives, he/she/it does live *or* he/she/it is living - **vive**

PLUR. We live, we do live *or* we are living - **vivimos**
You live, you do live *or* you are living - **vivís** (fam.), - **Ustedes viven** (form.)
They live, they do live *or* they are living - **viven**

Future

SING. I shall live - **viviré**
You will live **vivirás** (fam.), - **Usted vivirá** (form.)
He/she/it will live - **vivirá**

PLUR. We shall live - **viviremos**
You will live - **viviréis** (fam.), - **Ustedes vivirán** (form.)
They will live - **vivirán**

Past (Preterit)

SING. I lived *or* I did live - **viví**
You lived *or* you did live - **viviste** (fam.), - **Usted vivió** (form.)
He/she/it lived *or* he/she/it did live - **vivió**

PLUR. We lived *or* we did live - **vivimos**
You lived *or* you did live - **vivisteis** (fam.), - **Ustedes vivieron** (form.)
They lived *or* they did live - **vivieron**

Past (Indefinite)

SING. I have lived - **he vivido**
You have lived - **has vivido** (fam.), - **Usted ha vivido** (form.)
He/she/it has lived - **ha vivido**

PLUR. We have lived - **hemos vivido**
You have lived - **habéis vivido** (fam.), - **Ustedes han vivido** (form.)
They have lived - **han vivido**

Past (Imperfect *or* Continuous)

SING. I was living *or* I used to live - **vivía**
You were living *or* you used to live - **vivías** (fam.), - **Usted vivía** (form.)
He/she/it was living *or* he/she/it used to live - **vivía**

PLUR. We were living *or* we used to live - **vivíamos**
You were living *or* you used to live - **vivíais** (fam.), - **Ustedes vivían** (form.)
They were living *or* they used to live - **vivían**

Gerund

Living - **viviendo**

To Look - **Mirar**
(Also to Watch)
(Not to be confused with To Seem or To Appear - **Parecer**)

Present

SING. I look, I do look *or* I am looking - **miro**
You look, you do look *or* you are looking **miras** (fam.), - **Usted mira** (form.)
He/she/it looks, he/she/it does look *or* he/she/it is looking - **mira**

PLUR. We look, we do look *or* we are looking - **miramos**
You look, you do look *or* you are looking **miráis** (fam.), - **Ustedes miran** (form.)
They look, they do look, *or* they are looking - **miran**

Future

SING. I shall look - **miraré**
You will look - **mirarás** (fam.), - **Usted mirará** (form.)
He/she/it will look - **mirará**

PLUR. We shall look - **miraremos**
You will look - **miraréis** (fam.), - **Ustedes mirarán** (form.)
They will look - **mirarán**

Past (Preterit)

SING. I looked *or* I did look - **miré**
You looked *or* you did look - **miraste** (fam.), - **Usted miró** (form.)
He/she/it looked *or* he/she/it did look - **miró**

PLUR. We looked *or* we did look - **miramos**
You looked *or* you did look - **mirasteis** (fam.), - **Ustedes miraron** (form.)
They looked *or* they did look - **miraron**

Past (Indefinite)

SING. I have looked - **he mirado**
You have looked - **has mirado** (fam.), - **Usted ha mirado** (form.)
He/she/it has looked - **ha mirado**

PLUR. We have looked - **hemos mirado**
You have looked - **habéis mirado** (fam.), - **Ustedes han mirado** (form.)
They have looked - **han mirado**

Past (Imperfect *or* Continuous)

SING. I was looking *or* I used to look - **miraba**
You were looking *or* you used to look - **mirabas** (fam.), - **Usted miraba** (form.)
He/she/it was looking *or* he/she/it used to look - **miraba**

PLUR. We were looking *or* we used to look - **mirábamos**
You were looking *or* you used to look - **mirabais** (fam.), - **Ustedes miraban** (form.)
They were looking *or* they used to look - **miraban**

Gerund

Looking - **mirando**

To Look For - **Buscar**

(Boo-scar)

(Also To Seek or to go and get something, a much used and useful verb)

Present

SING. I am looking for - **busco**
You are looking for - **buscas** (fam.), - **Usted busca** (form.)
He/she/it is looking for - **busca**

PLUR. We are looking for - **buscamos**
You are looking for - **buscáis** (fam.), - **Ustedes buscan** (form.)
They are looking for - **buscan**

Future

SING. I shall look for - **buscaré**
You will look for - **buscarás** (fam.), - **Usted buscará** (form.)
He/she/it will look for - **buscará**

PLUR. We shall look for - **buscaremos**
You will look for - **buscaréis** (fam.), - **Ustedes buscarán** (form.)
They will look for - **buscarán**

Past (Preterit)

SING. I looked for - **busqué**
You looked for - **buscaste** (fam.), - **Usted buscó** (form.)
He/she/it looked for - **buscó**

PLUR. We looked for - **buscamos**
You looked for - **buscasteis** (fam.), - **Ustedes buscaron** (form.)
They looked for - **buscaron**

Past (Indefinite)

SING. I have looked for - **he buscado**
You have looked for - **has buscado** (fam.), - **Usted ha buscado** (form.)
He/she/it has looked for - **ha buscado**

PLUR. We have looked for - **hemos buscado**
You have looked for - **habéis buscado** (fam.), - **Ustedes han buscado** (form.)
They have looked for - **han buscado**

Past (Imperfect *or* Continuous)

SING. I was looking for *or* I used to look for - **buscaba**
You were looking for *or* you used to look for - **buscabas** (fam.), - **Usted buscaba** (form.)
He/she/it was looking for *or* he/she/it used to look for - **buscaba**

PLUR. We were looking for *or* we used to look for - **buscábamos**
You were looking for *or* you used to look for - **buscabais** (fam.), - **Ustedes buscaban** (form.)
They were looking for *or* they used to look for - **buscaban**

Gerund

Looking for - **buscando**

To Lose - **Perder**
(*Per-dair*)

Present

SING. I lose, I do lose *or* I am losing - **pierdo**
You lose, you do lose *or* you are losing - **pierdes** (fam.), - **Usted pierde** (form.)
He/she/it loses, he/she/it does lose *or* he/she/it is losing - **pierde**

PLUR. We lose, we do lose *or* we are losing - **perdemos**
You lose, you do lose *or* you are losing - **perdéis** (fam.), - **Ustedes pierden** (form.)
They lose, they do lose *or* they are losing - **pierden**

Future

SING. I shall lose - **perderé**
You will lose - **perderás** (fam.), - **Usted perderá** (form.)
He/she/it will lose - **perderá**

PLUR. We shall lose - **perderemos**
You will lose - **perderéis** (fam.), - **Ustedes perderán** (form.)
They will lose - **perderán**

Past (Preterit)

SING. I lost *or* I did lose - **perdí**
You lost *or* you did lose - **perdiste** (fam.), - **Usted perdió** (form.)
He/she/it lost *or* he/she/it did lose - **perdió**

PLUR. We lost *or* we did lose - **perdimos**
You lost *or* you did lose - **perdisteis** (fam.), **Ustedes perdieron** (form.)
They lost *or* they did lose - **perdieron**

Past (Indefinite)

SING. I have lost - **he perdido**
You have lost - **has perdido** (fam.), - **Usted ha perdido** (form.)
He/she/it has lost - **ha perdido**

PLUR. We have lost - **hemos perdido**
You have lost - **habéis perdido** (fam.), - **Ustedes han perdido** (form.)
They have lost - **han perdido**

Past (Imperfect *or* Continuous)

SING. I was losing *or* I used to lose - **perdía**
You were losing *or* you used to lose - **perdías** (fam.), - **Usted perdía** (form.)
He/she/it was losing *or* he/she/it used to lose - **perdía**

PLUR. We were losing *or* we used to lose - **perdíamos**
You were losing *or* you used to lose - **perdíais** (fam.), - **Ustedes perdían** (form.)
They were losing *or* they used to lose - **perdían**

Gerund

Losing - **perdiendo**

To Meet With (Or Encounter) - **Hallar**
(*Aye-yar*)

Present

SING. I meet, I do meet *or* I am meeting - **hallo**
You meet, you do meet *or* you are meeting - **hallas** (fam.), - **Usted halla** (form.)
He/she/it meets, he/she/it does meet *or* he/she/it is meeting - **halla**

PLUR. We meet, we do meet *or* we are meeting - **hallamos**
You meet, you do meet *or* you are meeting - **halláis** (fam.), - **Ustedes hallan** (form.)
They meet, they do meet *or* they are meeting - **hallan**

Future

SING. I shall meet - **hallaré**
You will meet - **hallarás** (fam.), - **Usted hallará** (form.)
He/she/it will meet - **hallará**

PLUR. We shall meet - **hallaremos**
You will meet - **hallaréis** (fam.), - **Ustedes hallarán** (form.)
They will meet - **hallarán**

Past (Preterit)

SING. I met *or* I did meet - **hallé**
You met *or* you did meet - **hallaste** (fam.), - **Usted halló** (form.)
He/she/it met *or* he/she/it did meet - **halló**

PLUR. We met *or* we did meet - **hallamos**
You met *or* you did meet - **hallasteis** (fam.), - **Ustedes hallaron** (form.)
They met *or* they did meet - **hallaron**

Past (Indefinite)

SING. I have met - **he hallado**
You have met - **has hallado** (fam.), - **Usted ha hallado** (form.)
He/she/it has met - **ha hallado**

PLUR. We have met - **hemos hallado**
You have met - **habéis hallado** (fam.), - **Ustedes han hallado** (form.)
They have met - **han hallado**

Past (Imperfect *or* Continuous)

SING. I was meeting *or* I used to meet - **hallaba**
You were meeting *or* you used to meet - **hallabas** (fam.), - **Usted hallaba** (form.)
He/she/it was meeting *or* he/she/it used to meet - **hallaba**

PLUR. We were meeting *or* we used to meet - **hallábamos**
You were meeting *or* you used to meet - **hallabais** (fam.), - **Ustedes hallaban** (form.)
They were meeting *or* they used to meet - **hallaban**

Gerund

Meeting - **hallando**

To Move - **Mover**
(*Mow-vair*)

Present

SING. I move, I do move *or* I am moving - **yo muevo**
You move, you do move *or* you are moving - **tú mueves** (fam.), - **Usted mueve** (form.)
He/she/it moves, he/she/it does move *or* he/she/it is moving - **mueve**

PLUR. We move, we do move *or* we are moving - **movemos**
You move, you do move *or* you are moving - **movéis** (fam.), - **Ustedes mueven** (form.)
They move, they do move *or* they are moving - **mueven**

Future

SING. I shall move - **moveré**
You will move - **moverás** (fam.), - **Usted moverá** (form.)
He/she/it will move - **moverá**

PLUR. We shall move - **moveremos**
You will move - **moveréis** (fam.), - **Ustedes moverán** (form.)
They will move - **moverán**

Past (Preterit)

SING. I moved *or* I did move - **moví**
You moved *or* you did move - **moviste** (fam.), - **Usted movió** (form.)
He/she/it moved *or* he/she/it did move - **movió**

PLUR. We moved *or* we did move - **movimos**
You moved *or* you did move - **movisteis** (fam.), - **Ustedes movieron** (form.)
They moved *or* they did move - **movieron**

Past (Indefinite)

SING. I have moved - **he movido**
You have moved - **has movido** (fam.), - **Usted ha movido** (form.)
He/she/it has moved - **ha movido**

PLUR. We have moved - **hemos movido**
You have moved - **habéis movido** (fam.), - **Ustedes han movido** (form.)
They have moved - **han movido**

Past (Imperfect *or* Continuous)

SING. I was moving *or* I used to move - **movía**
You were moving *or* you used to move - **movías** (fam.), - **Usted movía** (form.)
He/she/it was moving *or* he/she/it used to move - **movía**

PLUR. We were moving *or* we used to move - **movíamos**
You were moving *or* you used to move - **movíais** (fam.), - **Ustedes movían** (form.)
They were moving *or* they used to move - **movían**

Gerund

Moving - **moviendo**

To Need - **Necesitar**

Present

SING. I need, I do need *or* I am needing - **necesito**
You need, you do need *or* you are needing - **necesitas** (fam.), - **Usted necesita** (form.)
He/she/it needs, he/she/it does need *or* he/she/it is needing - **necesita**

PLUR. We need, we do need *or* we are needing - **necesitamos**
You need, you do need *or* you are needing - **necesitáis** (fam.), - **Ustedes necesitan** (form.)
They need, they do need *or* they are needing - **necesitan**

Future

SING. I shall need - **necesitaré**
You will need - **necesitarás** (fam.), - **Usted necesitará** (form.)
He/she/it will need - **necesitará**

PLUR. We shall need - **necesitaremos**
You will need - **necesitaréis** (fam.), - **Ustedes necesitarán** (form.)
They will need - **necesitarán**

Past (Preterit)

SING. I needed *or* I did need - **necesité**
You needed *or* you did need - **necesitaste** (fam.) - **Usted necesitó** (form.)
He/she/it needed *or* he/she/it did need - **necesitó**

PLUR. We needed *or* we did need - **necesitamos**
You needed *or* you did need - **necesitasteis** (fam.) - **Ustedes necesitaron** (form.)
They needed *or* they did need - **necesitaron**

Past (Indefinite)

SING. I have needed - **he necesitado**
You have needed - **has necesitado** (fam.), - **Usted ha necesitado** (form.)
He/she/it has needed - **ha necesitado**

PLUR. We have needed - **hemos necesitado**
You have needed - **habéis necesitado** (fam.), - **Ustedes han necesitado** (form.)
They have needed - **han necesitado**

Past (Imperfect *or* Continuous)

SING. I was needing *or* I used to need - **necesitaba**
You were needing *or* you used to need - **necesitabas** (fam.), - **Usted necesitaba** (form.)
He/she/it was needing *or* he/she/it used to need - **necesitaba**

PLUR. We were needing *or* we used to need - **necesitábamos**
You were needing *or* you used to need - **necesitabais** (fam.), - **Ustedes necesitaban** (form.)
They were needing *or* they used to need - **necestiban**

Gerund

Needing - **necesitando**

To Open - **Abrir**
(*Ab-rear*)

Present

SING. I open, I do open *or* I am opening - **abro**
You open, you do open *or* you are opening - **abres** (fam.), - **Usted abre** (form.)
He/she/it opens, he/she/it does open *or* he/she/it is opening - **abre**

PLUR. We open, we do open *or* we are opening - **abrimos**
You open, you do open *or* you are opening - **abrís** (fam.), - **Ustedes abren** (form.)
They open, they do open *or* they are opening - **abren**

Future

SING. I shall open - **abriré**
You will open - **abrirás** (fam.), - **Usted abrirá** (form.)
He/she/it will open - **abrirá**

PLUR. We shall open - **abriremos**
You will open - **abriréis** (fam.), - **Ustedes abrirán** (form.)
They will open - **abriŕan**

Past (Preterit)

SING. I opened *or* I did open - **abrí**
You opened *or* you did open - **abriste** (fam.), - **Usted abrió** (form.)
He/she/it opened *or* he/she/it did open - **abrió**

PLUR. We opened *or* we did open - **abrimos**
You opened *or* you did open - **abristeis** (fam.), - **Ustedes abrieron** (form.)
They opened *or* they did open - **abrieron**

Past (Indefinite)

SING. I have opened - **he abierto**
You have opened - **has abierto** (fam.), - **Usted ha abierto** (form.)
He/she/it has opened - **ha abierto**

PLUR. We have opened - **hemos abierto**
You have opened - **habéis abierto** (fam.), - **Ustedes han abierto** (form.)
They have opened - **han abierto**

Past (Imperfect *or* Continuous)

SING. I was opening *or* I used to open - **abría**
You were opening *or* you used to open - **abriás** (fam.), - **Usted abría** (form.)
He/she/it was opening *or* he/she/it used to open - **abría**

PLUR. We were opening *or* we used to open - **abríamos**
You were opening *or* you used to open - **abríais** (fam.), - **Ustedes abrian** (form.)
They were opening *or* they used to open - **abrian**

Gerund

Opening - **abriendo**

To Owe - **Deber**
(Deb-air)

(Also used where we use the words "should" and "ought")

Present

SING. I owe, I do owe *or* I am owing - **debo**
You owe, you do owe *or* you are owing - **debes** (fam.), - **Usted debe** (form.)
He/she/it owes, he/she/it does owe *or* he/she/it is owing - **debe**

PLUR. We owe, we do owe *or* we are owing - **debemos**
You owe, you do owe *or* you are owing - **debéis** (fam.), - **Ustedes deben** (form.)
They owe, they do owe *or* they are owing - **deben**

Future

SING. I shall owe - **deberé**
You will owe - **deberás** (fam.), - **Usted deberá** (form.)
He/she/it will owe - **deberá**

PLUR. We shall owe - **deberemos**
You will owe - **deberéis** (fam.), - **Ustedes deberán** (form.)
They will owe - **deberán**

Past (Preterit)

SING. I owed *or* I did owe - **debí**
You owed *or* you did owe - **debiste** (fam.), - **Usted debió** (form.)
He/she/it owed *or* he/she/it did owe - **debió**

PLUR. We owed *or* we did owe - **debimos**
You owed *or* you did owe - **debisteis** (fam.), - **Ustedes debieron** (form.)
They owed *or* they did owe - **debieron**

Past (Indefinite)

SING. I have owed - **he debido**
You have owed - **has debido** (fam.), - **Usted ha debido** (form.)
He/she/it has owed - **ha debido**

PLUR. We have owed - **hemos debido**
You have owed - **habéis debido** (fam.), - **Ustedes han debido** (form.)
They have owed - **han debido**

Past (Imperfect *or* Continuous)

SING. I was owing *or* I used to owe - **debía**
You were owing *or* you used to owe - **debías** (fam.), - **Usted debía** (form.)
He/she/it was owing *or* he/she/it used to owe - **debía**

PLUR. We were owing *or* we used to owe - **debíamos**
You were owing *or* you used to owe - **debíais** (fam.), - **Ustedes debían** (form).
They were owing *or* they used to owe - **debían**

Gerund

Owing - **debiendo**

To Pay - **Pagar**

Present

SING. I pay, I do pay *or* I am paying - **yo pago**
You pay, you do pay *or* you are paying - **pagas** (fam.), - **Usted paga** (form.)
He/she/it pays, he/she/it does pay *or* he/she/it is paying - **paga**

PLUR. We pay, we do pay *or* we are paying - **pagamos**
You pay, you do pay *or* you are paying - **pagáis** (fam.), - **Ustedes pagan** (form.)
They pay, they do pay *or* they are paying - **pagan**

Future

SING. I shall pay - **pagaré**
You will pay - **pagarás** (fam.), - **Usted pagará** (form.)
He/she/it will pay - **pagará**

PLUR. We shall pay - **pagaremos**
You will pay - **pagaréis** (fam.), - **Ustedes pagarán** (form.)
They will pay - **pagarán**

Past (Preterit)

SING. I paid *or* I did pay - **pagué**
You paid *or* you did pay - **pagaste** (fam.), - **Usted pagó** (form.)
He/she/it paid *or* he/she/it did pay - **pagó**

PLUR. We paid *or* we did pay **pagamos**
You paid *or* you did pay - **pagasteis** (fam.), - **Ustedes pagaron** (form.)
They paid *or* they did pay - **pagaron**

Past (Indefinite)

SING. I have paid - **he pagado**
You have paid - **has pagado** (fam.), - **Usted ha pagado** (form.)
He/she/it has paid - **ha pagado**

PLUR. We have paid - **hemos pagado**
You have paid - **habéis pagado** (fam.), - **Ustedes han pagado** (form.)
They have paid - **han pagado**

Past (Imperfect *or* Continuous)

SING. I was paying *or* I used to pay - **pagaba**
You were paying *or* you used to pay - **pagabas** (fam.), - **Usted pagaba** (form.)
He/she/it was paying *or* he/she/it used to pay - **pagaba**

PLUR. We were paying *or* we used to pay - **pagábamos**
You were paying *or* you used to pay - **pagabais** (fam.), - **Ustedes pagaban** (form.)
They were paying *or* they used to pay - **pagaban**

Gerund

Paying - **pagando**

To Play - **Jugar**
(Hoo-gar)

(But not to play a musical instrument,for this see **Tocar**, page 98)

Present

SING. I play, I do play *or* I am playing - **juego**
You, play, you do play *or* you are playing - **juegas** (fam.), - **Usted juega** (form.)
He/she/it plays, he/she/it does play *or* he/she/it is playing - **juega**

PLUR. We play, we do play *or* we are playing - **jugamos**
You play, you do play *or* you are playing - **jugáis** (fam.), - **Ustedes juegan** (form.)
They play, they do play *or* they are playing - **juegan**

Future

SING. I shall play - **jugaré**
You will play - **jugarás** (fam.), - **Usted jugará** (form.)
He/she/it will play - **jugará**

PLUR. We shall play - **jugaremos**
You will play - **jugaréis** (fam.), - **Ustedes jugarán** (form.)
They will play - **jugarán**

Past (Preterit)

SING. I played *or* I did play - **jugué**
You played *or* you did play - **jugaste** (fam.), - **Usted jugó** (form.)
He/she/it played *or* he/she/it did play - **jugó**

PLUR. We played *or* we did play - **jugamos**
You played *or* you did play - **jugasteis** (fam.), - **Ustedes jugaron** (form.)
They played *or* they did play - **jugaron**

Past (Indefinite)

SING. I have played - **he jugado**
You have played - **has jugado** (fam.), - **Usted ha jugado** (form.)
He/she/it has played - **ha jugado**

PLUR. We have played - **hemos jugado**
You have played - **habéis jugado** (fam.), - **Ustedes han jugado** (form.)
They have played - **han jugado**

Past (Imperfect *or* Continuous)

SING. I was playing *or* I used to play - **jugaba**
You were playing *or* you used to play - **jugabas** (fam.), - **Usted jugaba** (form.)
He/she/it was playing *or* he/she/it used to play - **jugaba**

PLUR. We were playing *or* we used to play - **jugábamos**
You were playing *or* you used to play - **jugabais** (fam.), - **Ustedes jugaban** (form.)
They were playing *or* they used to play - **jugaban**

Gerund

Playing - **jugando**

To Pour - **Echar**
(Also **Verter** but **Echar** is more commonly used)

Present

SING. I pour, I do pour *or* I am pouring - **echo**
You pour, you do pour *or* you are pouring - **echas** (fam.), - **Usted echa** (form.)
He/she/it pours, he/she/it does pour *or* he/she/it is pouring - **echa**

PLUR. We pour, we do pour *or* we are pouring - **echamos**
You pour, you do pour *or* you are pouring - **echais** (fam.), - **Ustedes echan** (form.)
They pour, they do pour *or* they are pouring - **echan**

Future

SING. I shall pour - **echaré**
You will pour - **echarás** (fam.), - **Usted echará** (form.)
He/she/it will pour - **echará**

PLUR. We shall pour - **echaremos**
You will pour - **echaréis** (fam.), - **Ustedes echarán** (form.)
They will pour - **echarán**

Past (Preterit)

SING. I poured *or* I did pour - **eché**
You poured *or* you did pour - **echaste** (fam.), - **Usted echó** (form.)
He/she/it poured *or* he/she/it did pour - **echó**

PLUR. We poured *or* we did pour - **echamos**
You poured *or* you did pour - **echasteis** (fam.), - **Ustedes echaron** (form.)
They poured *or* they did pour - **echaron**

Past (Indefinite)

SING. I have poured - **he echado**
You have poured - **has echado** (fam.), - **Usted ha echado** (form.)
He/she/it has poured - **ha echado**

PLUR. We have poured - **hemos echado**
You have poured - **habéis echado** (fam.), - **Ustedes han echado** (form.)
They have poured - **han echado**

Past (Imperfect *or* Continuous)

SING. I was pouring *or* I used to pour - **echaba**
You were pouring *or* you used to pour - **echabas** (fam.), - **Usted echaba** (form.)
He/she/it was pouring *or* he/she/it used to pour - **echaba**

PLUR. We were pouring *or* we used to pour - **echábamos**
You were pouring *or* you used to pour - **echabais** (fam.), - **Ustedes echaban** (form.)
They were pouring *or* they used to pour - **echaban**

Gerund

Pouring - **echando**

To Prefer - **Preferir**

Present

SING. I prefer *or* I do prefer - **prefiero**
You prefer *or* you do prefer - **prefieres** (fam.), - **Usted prefiere** (form.)
He/she/it prefers *or* he/she/it does prefer - **prefiere**

PLUR.We prefer *or* we do prefer - **preferimos**
You prefer *or* you do prefer - **preferís** (fam.), - **Ustedes prefieren** (form.)
They prefer *or* theydo prefer - **prefieren**

Future

SING. I shall prefer - **preferiré**
You will prefer - **preferirás** (fam.), - **Usted preferirá** (form.)
He/she/it will prefer - **preferirá**

PLUR. We shall prefer - **preferiremos**
You will prefer - **preferís** (fam.), - **Ustedes prefieren** (form.)
They will prefer - **preferiŕan**

Past (Preterit)

SING. I preferred *or* I did prefer - **preferí**
You preferred *or* you did prefer - **preferiste** (fam.), - **Usted prefirió** (form.)
He/she/it preferred *or* he/she/it did prefer - **prefirió**

PLUR. We preferred *or* we did prefer - **preferimos**
You preferred *or* you did prefer - **preferisteis** (fam.), - **Ustedes prefirieron** (form.)
They preferred *or* they did prefer - **prefirieron**

Past (Indefinite)

SING. I have preferred - **he preferido**
You have preferred - **has preferido** (fam.), - **Usted ha preferido** (form.)
He/she/it has preferred - **ha preferido**

PLUR. We have preferred - **hemos preferido**
You have preferred - **habéis preferido** (fam.), - **Ustedes han preferido** (form.)
They have preferred - **han preferido**

Past (Imperfect *or* Continuous)

SING. I used to prefer - **prefería**
You used to prefer - **preferías** (fam.), - **Usted prefería** (form.)
He/she/it used to prefer - **prefería**

PLUR. We used to prefer - **preferíamos**
You used to prefer - **preferíais** (fam.), - **Ustedes preferían** (form.)
They used to prefer - **preferían**

Gerund

Preferring - **prefiriendo**

To Provide - **Proveer**
(*Prov-ay-air*)

Present

SING. I provide, I do provide *or* I am providing - **proveo**
You provide, you do provide *or* you are providing - **provees** (fam.), - **Usted provee** (form.)
He/she/it provides, he/she/it does provide *or* he/she/it is providing - **provee**

PLUR. We provide, we do provide *or* we are providing - **proveemos**
You provide, you do provide *or* you are providing - **proveéis** (fam.) - **Ustedes proveen** (form.)
They provide, they do provide *or* they are providing - **proveen**

Future

SING. I shall provide - **proveeré**
You will provide - **proveerás** (fam.), - **Usted proveerá** (form.)
He/she/it will provide - **proveerá**

PLUR. We shall provide - **proveeremos**
You will provide - **proveeréis** (fam.), - **Ustedes proveerán** (form.)
They will provide - **proveerán**

Past (Preterit)

SING. I provided *or* I did provide - **proveí**
You provided *or* you did provide - **proveíste** (fam.), - **Usted proveyó** (form.)
He/she/it provided *or* he/she/it did provide - **proveyó**

PLUR. We provided *or* we did provide - **proveímos**
You provided *or* you did provide - **proveísteis** (fam.), - **Ustedes proveyeron** (form.)
They provided *or* they did provide - **preveyeron**

Past (Indefinite)

SING. I have provided - **he proveído**
You have provided - **has proveído** (fam.), - **Usted ha proveído** (form.)
He/she/it has provided - **ha proveído**

PLUR. We have provided - **hemos proveído**
You have provided - **habéis proveído** (fam.), - **Ustedes han proveído** (form.)
They have provided - **han proveído**

Past (Imperfect *or* Continuous)

SING. I was providing *or* I used to provide - **proveía**
You were providing *or* you used to provide - **proveías** (fam.), - **Usted proveía** (form.)
He/she/it was providing *or* he/she/it used to provide - **proveía**

PLUR. We were providing *or* we used to provide - **proveíamos**
You were providing *or* you used to provide - **proveíais** (fam.), - **Ustedes proveían**
(form.)
They were providing *or* they used to provide - **proveían**

Gerund

Providing - **proveyendo**

To Put (Also to Place) - **Poner**
(Pon-air)

Present

SING. I put, I do put *or* I am putting - **pongo**
You put, you do put *or* you are putting - **pones** (fam)., - **Usted pone** (form.)
He/she/it puts, he/she/it does put *or* it is putting - **pone**

PLUR. We put, we do put *or* we are putting - **ponemos**
You put, you do put *or* you are putting - **ponéis** (fam.), - **Ustedes ponen** (form.)
They put, they do put *or* they are putting - **ponen**

Future

SING. I shall put - **pondré**
You will put - **pondrás** (fam.), - **Usted pondrá** (form.)
He/she/it will put - **pondrá**

PLUR. We shall put - **pondremos**
You will put - **pondréis** (fam.), - **Ustedes pondrán** (form.)
They will put - **pondrán**

Past (Preterit)

SING. I put *or* I did put - **puse**
You put *or* you did put - **pusiste** (fam.), - **Usted puso** (form.)
He/she/it put *or* he/she/it did put - **puso**

PLUR. We put *or* we did put - **pusimos**
You put *or* you did put - **pusisteis** (fam.), - **Ustedes pusieron** (form.)
They put *or* they did put - **pusieron**

Past (Indefinite)

SING. I have put - **he puesto**
You have put - **has puesto** (fam.), - **Ustedes ha puesto** (form.)
He/she/it has put - **ha puesto**

PLUR. We have put - **hemos puesto**
You have put - **habéis puesto** (fam.), - **Ustedes han puesto** (form.)
They have put - **han puesto**

Past (Imperfect *or* Continuous)

SING. I was putting *or* I used to put - **ponía**
You were putting *or* you used to put - **ponías** (fam.), - **Usted ponía** (form.)
He/she/it was putting *or* he/she/it used to put - **ponía**

PLUR. We were putting *or* we used to put - **poníamos**
You were putting *or* you used to put - **poníais** (fam.), - **Ustedes ponían** (form.)
They were putting *or* they used to put - **ponían**

Gerund

Putting - **poniendo**

To Put On (Clothing) - **Ponerse**
(Pon-air-say)
(Also To Become, as to become sick)

Present

SING. I put on, I do put on *or* I am putting on - **me pongo**
You put on, you do put on *or* you are putting on - **te pones** (fam.), - **Usted se pone** (form.)
He/she/it puts on, he/she/it does put on *or* he/she/it is putting on - **se pone**

PLUR. We put on, we do put on *or* we are putting on - **nos ponemos**
You put on, you do put on *or* you are putting on - **os ponéis** (fam.), - **Ustedes se ponen** (form.)
They put on, they do put on *or* they are putting on - **se ponen**

Future

SING. I shall put on *or* I shall become - **me pondré**
You will put on *or* you will become - **te pondrás** (fam.), - **Usted se pondrá** (form.)
He/she/it will put on *or* he/she/it will become - **se pondrá**

PLUR. We shall put on *or* we shall become - **nos pondremos**
You will put on *or* you will become - **os pondréis** (fam.), - **Ustedes se pondrán** (form.)
They will put on *or* they will become - **se pondrán**

Past (Preterit)

SING. I did put on *or* I became - **me puse**
You did put on *or* you became - **te pusiste** (fam.), - **Usted se puso** (form).
He/she/it did put on *or* he/she/it became - **se puso**

PLUR. We did put on *or* we became - **nos pusimos**
You did put on *or* you became - **os pusisteis** (fam.), - **Ustedes se pusieron** (form.)
They did put on *or* they became - **se pusieron**

Past (Indefinite)

SING. I have put on *or* I have become - **me he puesto**
You have put on *or* you have become - **te has puesto** (fam.), - **Usted se ha puesto** (form.)
He/she/it has put on *or* he/she/it has become - **se ha puesto**

PLUR. We have put on *or* we have become - **nos hemos puesto**
You have put on *or* you have become - **os habéis puesto** (fam.), - **Ustedes se han puesto** (form.)
They have put on *or* they have become - **se han puesto**

Past (Imperfect *or* Continuous)

SING. I was becoming *or* I used to put on - **me ponía**
You were becoming *or* you used to put on - **te ponías** (fam.), - **Usted se ponía** (form.)
He/she/it was becoming *or* he/she/it used to put on - **se ponía**

PLUR. We were becoming *or* we used to put on - **nos poníamos**
You were becoming *or* you used to put on - **os poníais** (fam.), - **Ustedes se ponían** (form.)
They were becoming *or* they used to put on - **se ponían**

Gerund

Putting on *or* becoming - **poniéndose**

To Read - **Leer**
(Lay-air)

Present

SING. I read I do read *or* I am reading - **leo**
You read, you do read *or* you are reading - **lees** (fam.), - **Usted lee** (form.)
He/she/it reads, he/she/it does read *or* he/she/it is reading - **lee**

PLUR. We read, we do read *or* we are reading - **leemos**
You read, you do read *or* you are reading - **leéis** (fam.), - **Ustedes leen** (form.)
They read, they do read *or* they are reading - **leen**

Future

SING. I shall read - **leeré**
You will read - **leerás** (fam.), - **Usted leerá** (form.)
He/she/it will read - **leerá**

PLUR. We shall read - **leeremos**
You will read - **leeréis** (fam.), - **Ustedes leerán** (form.)
They will read - **leerán**

Past (Preterit)

SING. I read *or* I did read - **leí**
You read *or* you did read - **leíste** (fam.), - **Usted leyó** (form.)
He/she/it read *or* he/she/it did read - **leyó**

PLUR. We read *or* we did read - **leímos**
You read *or* you did read - **leísteis** (fam.), - **Ustedes leyeron** (form.)
They read *or* they did read - **leyeron**

Past (Indefinite)

SING. I have read - **he leído**
You have read - **has leído** (fam.), - **Usted ha leído** (form.)
He/she/it has read - **ha leído**

PLUR. We have read - **hemos leído**
You have read - **habéis leído** (fam.), - **Ustedes han leído** (form.)
They have read - **han leído**

Past (Imperfect *or* Continuous)

SING. I was reading *or* I used to read - **leía**
You were reading *or* you used to read - **leías** (fam.), - **Usted leía** (form.)
He/she/it was reading *or* he/she/it used to read - **leía**

PLUR. We were reading *or* we used to read - **leíamos**
You were reading *or* you used to read - **leíais** (fam.), - **Ustedes leían** (form.)
They were reading *or* they used to read - **leían**

Gerund

Reading - **leyendo**

To Remember - **Recordar**
(Also To Remind)

Present

SING. I remember, I do remember *or* I am remembering - **yo recuerdo**
You remember, you do remember *or* you are remembering - **tú recuerdas** (fam.), - **Usted recuerda** (form.)
He/she/it remembers, he/she/it does remember *or* he/she/it is remembering - **recuerda**

PLUR. We remember, we do remember *or* we are remembering - **recordamos**
You remember, you do remember *or* you are remembering - **recordáis** (fam.), - **Ustedes recuerdan** (form.)
They remember, they do remember *or* they are remembering - **recuerdan**

Future

SING. I shall remember - **recordaré**
You will remember - **recordarás** (fam.), - **Usted recordará** (form.)
He/she/it will remember - **recordará**

PLUR. We shall remember - **recordaremos**
You will remember - **recordaréis** (fam.), - **Ustedes recordarán** (form.)
They will remember - **recordarán**

Past (Preterit)

SING. I remembered *or* I did remember - **recordé**
You remembered *or* you did remember - **recordaste** (fam.), - **Usted recordó** (form.)
He/she/it remembered *or* he/she/it did remember - **recordó**

PLUR. We remembered *or* we did remember - **recordamos**
You remembered *or* you did remember - **recordasteis** (fam.), - **Ustedes recordaron** (form.)
They remembered *or* they did remember - **recordaron**

Past (Indefinite)

SING. I have remembered - **he recordado**
You have remembered - **has recordado** (fam.), - **Usted ha recordado** (form.)
He/she/it has remembered - **ha recordado**

PLUR. We have remembered - **hemos recordado**
You have remembered - **habéis recordado** (fam.), - **Ustedes han recordado** (form.)
They have remembered - **han recordado**

Past (Imperfect *or* Continuous)

SING. I was remembering *or* I used to remember - **recordaba**
You were remembering *or* you used to remember - **recordabas** (fam.), - **Usted recordaba** (form.)
He/she/it was remembering *or* he/she/it used to remember - **recordaba**

PLUR. We were remembering *or* we used to remember - **recordábamos**
You were remembering *or* you used to remember - **recordabais** (fam.), - **Ustedes recordaban** (form.)
They were remembering *or* they used to remember - **recordaban**

Gerund

Remembering - **recordando**

To Return - **Volver**
(Vol-vair)

Present

SING. I return, I do return *or* I am returning - **yo vuelvo**
You return, you do return *or* you are returning - **tú vuelves** (fam.), - **Usted vuelve** (form.)
He/she/it returns, he/she/it does return *or* he/she/it is returning - **vuelve**

PLUR. We return, we do return *or* we are returning - **volvemos**
You return, you do return *or* you are returning - **volvéis** (fam.), - **Ustedes vuelven** (form.)
They return, they do return *or* they are returning - **vuelven**

Future

SING. I shall return - **volveré**
You will return - **volverás** (fam.), - **Usted volverá** (form.)
He/she/it will return - **volverá**

PLUR. We shall return - **volveremos**
You will return - **volveréis** (fam.), - **Ustedes volverán** (form.)
They will return - **volverán**

Past (Preterit)

SING. I returned *or* I did return - **volví**
You returned *or* you did return - **volviste** (fam.), - **Usted volvió** (form.)
He/she/it returned *or* he/she/it did return - **volvió**

PLUR. We returned *or* we did return - **volvimos**
You returned *or* you did return - **volvisteis** (fam.), - **Ustedes volvieron** (form.)
They returned *or* they did return - **volvieron**

Past (Indefinite)

SING. I have returned - **he vuelto**
You have returned - **has vuelto** (fam.), - **Usted ha vuelto** (form.)
He/she/it has returned - **ha vuelto**

PLUR. We have returned - **hemos vuelto**
You have returned - **habéis vuelto** (fam.), - **Ustedes han vuelto** (form.)
They have returned - **han vuelto**

Past (Imperfect *or* Continuous)

SING. I was returning *or* I used to return - **volvía**
You were returning *or* you used to return - **volvías** (fam.), - **Usted volvía** (form.)
He/she/it was returning *or* he/she/it used to return - **volvía**

PLUR. We were returning *or* we used to return - **volvíamos**
You were returning *or* you used to return - **volvíais** (fam.), - **Ustedes volvían** (form.)
They were returning *or* they used to return - **volvían**

Gerund

Returning - **volviendo**

To Say - **Decir**
(Deth-ear)
(Also To Tell)

Present

SING. I say, I do say *or* I am saying - **yo digo**
You say, you do say *or* you are saying - **tú dices** (fam.), - **Usted dice** (form.)
He/she/it says, he/she/it does say *or* he/she/it is saying - **dice**

PLUR. We say, we do say *or* we are saying - **decimos**
You say, you do say *or* you are saying - **decís** (fam.), - **Ustedes dicen** (form.)
They say, they do say *or* they are saying - **dicen**

Future

SING. I shall say - **diré**
You will say - **dirás** (fam.), - **Usted dirá** (form.)
He/she/it will say - **dirá**

PLUR. We shall say - **diremos**
You will say - **diréis** (fam.), - **Ustedes dirán** (form.)
They will say - **dirán**

Past (Preterit)

SING. I said *or* I did say - **dije**
You said *or* you did say - **dijiste** (fam.), - **Usted dijo** (form.)
He/she/it said *or* he/she/it did say - **dijo**

PLUR. We said *or* we did say - **dijimos**
You said *or* you did say - **dijisteis** (fam.), - **Ustedes dijeron** (form.)
They said *or* they did say - **dijeron**

Past (Indefinite)

SING. I have said - **he dicho**
You have said - **has dicho** (fam.), - **Usted ha dicho** (form.)
He/she/it has said - **ha dicho**

PLUR. We have said - **hemos dicho**
You have said - **habéis dicho** (fam.), - **Ustedes han dicho** (form.)
They have said - **han dicho**

Past (Imperfect *or* Continuous)

SING. I was saying *or* I used to say - **decía**
You were saying *or* you used to say - **decías** (fam.), - **Usted decía** (form.)
He/she/it was saying *or* he/she/it used to say - **decía**

PLUR. We were saying *or* we used to say - **decíamos**
You were saying *or* you used to say - **decíais** (fam.), - **Ustedes decían** (form.)
They were saying *or* they used to say - **decían**

Gerund

Saying - **diciendo**

To See - **Ver**
(Vair)

Present

SING. I see, I do see *or* I am seeing - **yo veo**
You see, you do see *or* you are seeing - **tú ves** (fam.), - **Usted ve** (form.)
He/she/it sees, he/she/it does see *or* he/she/it is seeing - **ve**

PLUR. We see, we do see *or* we are seeing - **vemos**
You see, you do see *or* you are seeing - **veis** (fam.), - **Ustedes ven** (form.)
They see, they do see *or* they are seeing - **ven**

Future

SING. I shall see - **veré**
You will see - **verás** (fam.), - **Usted verá** (form.)
He/she/it will see - **verá**

PLUR. We shall see - **veremos**
You will see - **veréis** (fam.), - **Ustedes verán** (form.)
They will see - **verán**

Past (Preterit)

SING. I saw *or* I did see - **yo vi**
You saw *or* you did see - **viste** (fam.), - **Usted vio** (form.)
He/she/it saw *or* he/she/it did see - **vio**

PLUR. We saw *or* we did see - **vimos**
You saw *or* you did see - **visteis** (fam.), - **Ustedes vieron** (form.)
They saw *or* they did see - **vieron**

Past (Indefinite)

SING. I have seen - **he visto**
You have seen - **has visto** (fam.), - **Usted ha visto** (form.)
He/she/it has seen - **ha visto**

PLUR. We have seen - **hemos visto**
You have seen - **habéis visto** (fam.), - **Ustedes han visto** (form.)
They have seen - **han visto**

Past (Imperfect *or* Continuous)

SING. I was seeing *or* I used to see - **veía**
You were seeing *or* you used to see - **veías** (fam.), - **Usted veía** (form.)
He/she/it was seeing *or* he/she/it used to see - **veía**

PLUR. We were seeing *or* we used to see - **veíamos**
You were seeing *or* you used to see - **veíais** (fam.), - **Ustedes veían** (form.)
They were seeing *or* they used to see - **veían**

Gerund

Seeing - **viendo**

To Seem or To Appear - **Parecer**
(Par-eth-air)
(For To Appear, i.e. come into view the verb is **Aparecer)**

Present

SING. I seem *or* I do seem - **parezco**
You seem *or* you do seem - **pareces** (fam.), - **Usted parece** (form.)
He/she/it seems *or* he/she/it does seem - **parece**

PLUR. We seem *or* we do seem - **parecemos**
You seem *or* you do seem - **parecéis** (fam.), - **Ustedes parecen** (form.)
They seem *or* they do seem - **parecen**

Future

SING. I shall seem - **pareceré**
You will seem - **parecerás** (fam.), - **Usted parecerá** (form.)
He/she/it will seem - **parecerá**

PLUR. We shall seem - **pareceremos**
You will seem - **pareceréis** (fam.), - **Ustedes parecerán** (form.)
They will seem - **parecerán**

Past (Preterit)

SING. I seemed *or* I did seem - **parecí**
You seemed *or* you did seem - **pareciste** (fam.), - **Usted pareció** (form.)
He/she/it seemed *or* he/she/it did seem - **pareció**

PLUR. We seemed *or* you did seem - **parecimos**
You seemed *or* you did seem - **parecisteis** (fam.), - **Ustedes parecieron** (form.)
They seemed *or* they did seem - **parecieron**

Past (Indefinite)

SING. I have seemed - **he parecido**
You have seemed - **has parecido** (fam.), - **Usted ha parecido** (form.)
He/she/it has seemed - **ha parecido**

PLUR. We have seemed - **hemos parecido**
You have seemed - **habeis parecido** (fam.), - **Ustedes han parecido** (form.)
They have seemed - **han parecido**

Past (Imperfect *or* Continuous)

SING. I used to seem - **parecía**
You used to seem - **parecias** (fam.), - **Usted parecia** (form.)
He/she/it used to seem - **parecía**

PLUR. We used to seem - **parecíamos**
You used to seem - **parecíais** (fam.), - **Ustedes parecían** (form.)
They used to seem - **parecían**

Gerund

Seeming *or* Appearing - **pareciendo**

To Sell - **Vender**
(*Ven-dair*)

Present

SING. I sell, I do sell *or* I am selling - **vendo**
You sell, you do sell *or* you are selling - **vendes** (fam.),- **Usted vende** (form.)
He/she/it sells, he/she/it does sell *or* he/she/it is selling - **vende**

PLUR. We sell, we do sell *or* we are selling - **vendemos**
You sell, you do sell *or* you are selling - **vendéis** (fam.), - **Ustedes venden** (form.)
They sell they do sell *or* they are selling - **venden**

Future

SING. I shall sell - **venderé**
You will sell - **venderás** (fam.), - **Usted venderá** (form.)
He/she/it will sell - **venderá**

PLUR. We shall sell - **venderemos**
You will sell - **venderéis** (fam.), - **Ustedes venderán** (form.)
They will sell - **venderán**

Past (Preterit)

SING. I sold *or* I did sell - **vendí**
You sold *or* you did sell - **vendiste** (fam.), - **Usted vendió** (form.)
He/she/it sold *or* he/she/it did sell - **vendió**

PLUR. We sold *or* we did sell - **vendimos**
You sold *or* you did sell - **vendisteis** (fam.), - **Ustedes vendieron** (form.)
They sold *or* they did sell - **vendieron**

Past (Indefinite)

SING. I have sold - **he vendido**
You have sold - **has vendido** (fam.), - **Usted ha vendido (form.)**
He/she/it has sold - **ha vendido**

PLUR. We have sold - **hemos vendido**
You have sold - **habéis vendido** (fam.), - **Ustedes han vendido** (form.)
They have sold - **han vendido**

Past (Imperfect *or* Continuous)

SING. I was selling *or* I used to sell - **vendía**
You were selling *or* you used to sell - **vendías** (fam.), - **Usted vendía** (form.)
He/she/it was selling *or* he/she/it used to sell - **vendía**

PLUR. We were selling *or* we used to sell - **vendíamos**
You were selling *or* you used to sell - **vendíais** (fam.), - **Ustedes vendían** (form.)
They were selling *or* they used to sell - **vendían**

Gerund

Selling - **vendiendo**

To Send - **Mandar**
(Also **Enviar** but **Mandar** seems to be more commonly used)

Present

SING. I send, I do send *or* I am sending - **mando**
You send, you do send *or* you are sending - **mandas** (fam.), - **Usted manda** (form.)
He/she/it sends, he/she/it does send *or* he/she/it is sending - **manda**

PLUR. We send, we do send *or* we are sending - **mandamos**
You send, you do send *or* you are sending - **mandáis** (fam.), - **Ustedes mandan** (form.)
They send, they do send *or* they are sending - **mandan**

Future

SING. I shall send - **mandaré**
You will send - **mandarás** (fam.) - **Usted mandará** (form.)
He/she/it will send - **mandará**

PLUR. We shall send - **mandaremos**
You will send - **mandaréis** (fam.), - **Ustedes mandarán** (form.)
They will send - **mandarán**

Past (Preterit)

SING. I sent *or* I did send - **mandé**
You sent *or* you did send - **mandaste** (fam.), - **Usted mandó** (form.)
He/she/it sent *or* he/she/it did send - **mandó**

PLUR. We sent *or* we did send - **mandamos**
You sent *or* you did send - **mandasteis** (fam.), - **Ustedes mandaron** (form.)
They sent *or* they did send - **mandaron**

Past (Indefinite)

SING. I have sent - **he mandado**
You have sent - **has mandado** (fam.), - **Usted ha mandado** (form.)
He/she/it has sent - **ha mandado**

PLUR. We have sent - **hemos mandado**
You have sent - **habéis mandado** (fam.), - **Ustedes han mandado** (form.)
They have sent - **han mandado**

Past (Imperfect *or* Continuous)

SING. I was sending *or* I used to send - **mandaba**
You were sending *or* you used to send - **mandabas** fam.), - **Usted mandaba** (form.)
He/she/it was sending *or* he/she/it used to send - **mandaba**

PLUR. We were sending *or* we used to send - **mandábamos**
You were sending *or* you used to send - **mandabais** (fam.), - **Ustedes mandaban** (form.)
They were sending *or* they used to send - **mandaban**

Gerund

Sending - **mandando**

To Sit Down - **Sentarse**
(Sen-tar-say)
(To seat oneself)

Present

SING. I seat myself *or* I am seating myself - **me siento**
You seat yourself *or* you are seating yourself - **te sientas** (fam.), - **Usted se sienta** (form.)
He/she/it seats him/her/itself *or* he/she/it is seating him/her/itself - **se sienta**

PLUR. We seat ourselves *or* we are seating ourselves - **nos sentamos**
You seat yourselves *or* you are seating yourselves - **os sentáis** (fam.), - **Ustedes se sientan** (form.)
They seat themselves *or* they are seating themselves - **se sientan**

Future

SING. I shall seat myself - **me sentaré**
You will seat yourself - **te sentarás** (fam.), - **Usted se sentará** (form.)
He/she/it will seat him/her/itself - **se sentará**

PLUR. We shall seat ourselves - **nos sentaremos**
You will seat yourselves - **os sentaréis** (fam.), - **Ustedes se sentarán** (form.)
They will seat themselves - **se sentarán**

Past (Preterit)

SING. I sat myself *or* I did seat myself - **me senté**
You sat yourself *or* you did seat yourself - **te sentaste** (fam.), - **Usted se sentó** (form.)
He/she/it sat him/her/itself *or* he/she/it did seat him/her/itself - **se sentó**

PLUR. We sat ourselves *or* we did seat ourselves - **nos sentamos**
You sat yourselves *or* you did seat yourselves - **os sentasteis** (fam.), - **Ustedes se sentaron** (form.)
They sat themselves *or* they did seat themselves - **se sentaron**

Past (Indefinite)

SING. I have seated myself - **me he sentado**
You have seated yourself - **te has sentado** (fam.), - **Usted se ha sentado** (form.)
He/she/it has seated him/her/itself - **se ha sentado**

PLUR. We have seated ourselves - **nos hemos sentado**
You have seated yourselves - **os habéis sentado** (fam.), - **Ustedes se han sentado** (form.)
They have seated themselves - **se han sentado**

Past (Imperfect *or* Continuous)

SING. I was seating myself *or* I used to seat myself - **me sentaba**
You were seating yourself *or* you used to seat yourself - **te sentabas** (fam.), - **Usted se sentaba** (form.)
He/she/it was seating him/her/itself *or* he/she/it used to seat him/her/itself - **se sentaba**

PLUR. We were seating ourselves *or* we used to seat ourselves - **nos sentábamos**
You were seating yourselves *or* you used to seat yourselves - **os sentabais** (fam.), - **Ustedes se sentaban** (form.)
They were seating themselves *or* they used to seat themselves - **se sentaban**

Gerund

Seating oneself - **sentándose**

To Sleep - **Dormir**
(*Dorm-ear*)

Present

SING. I sleep, I do sleep *or* I am sleeping - **duermo**
You sleep, you do sleep *or* you are sleeping - **duermes** (fam.), - **Usted duerme** (form.)
He/she/it sleeps, he/she/it does sleep *or* he/she/it is sleeping - **duerme**

PLUR. We sleep, we do sleep *or* we are sleeping - **dormimos**
You sleep, you do sleep *or* you are sleeping - **dormís** (fam.), - **Ustedes duermen** (form.)
They sleep, they do sleep *or* they are sleeping - **duermen**

Future

SING. I shall sleep - **dormiré**
You will sleep - **dormirás** (fam.), - **Usted dormirá** (form.)
He/she/it will sleep - **dormirá**

PLUR. We shall sleep - **dormiremos**
You will sleep - **dormiréis** (fam.), - **Ustedes dormirán** (form.)
They will sleep - **dormirán**

Past (Preterit)

SING. I slept *or* I did sleep - **dormí**
You slept *or* you did sleep - **dormiste** (fam.), - **Usted durmió** (form.)
He/she/it slept *or* he/she/it did sleep - **durmió**

PLUR. We slept *or* we did sleep - **dormimos**
You slept *or* you did sleep - **dormisteis** (fam.), - **Ustedes durmieron** (form.)
They slept *or* they did sleep - **durmieron**

Past (Indefinite)

SING. I have slept - **he dormido**
You have slept - **has dormido** (fam.), - **Usted ha dormido** (form.)
He/she/it has slept - **ha dormido**

PLUR. We have slept - **hemos dormido**
You have slept - **habéis dormido** (fam.), - **Ustedes han dormido** (form.)
They have slept - **han dormido**

Past (Imperfect *or* Continuous)

SING. I was sleeping *or* I used to sleep - **dormía**
You were sleeping *or* you used to sleep - **dormías** (am.), - **Usted dormía** (form.)
He/she/it was sleeping *or* he/she/it used to sleep - **dormía**

PLUR. We were sleeping *or* we used to sleep - **dormíamos**
You were sleeping *or* you used to sleep - **dormíais** (fam.), - **Ustedes dormían** (form.)
They were sleeping *or* they used to sleep - **dormían**

Gerund

Sleeping - **durmiendo**

To Speak - **Hablar**
(Pronunciation: Drop the H)
Also to Talk

Present

SING. I speak, I do speak *or* I am speaking - **hablo**
You speak, you do speak *or* you are speaking - **hablas** (fam.), - **Usted habla** (form.)
He/she/it speaks, he/she/it does speak, *or* he/she/it is speaking - **habla**

PLUR. We speak, we do speak *or* we are speaking - **hablamos**
You speak, you do speak *or* you are speaking - **habláis** (fam.), - **Ustedes hablan** (form.)
They speak, they do speak *or* they are speaking - **hablan**

Future

SING. I shall speak - **hablaré**
You will speak - **hablarás** (fam.), - **Usted hablará** (form.)
He/she/it will speak - **hablará**

PLUR. We shall speak - **hablaremos**
You will speak - **hablaréis** (fam.), - **Ustedes hablarán** (form.)
They will speak - **hablarán**

Past (Preterit)

SING. I spoke *or* I did speak - **hablé**
You spoke *or* you did speak - **hablaste** (fam.), - **Usted habló** (form.)
He/she/it spoke *or* he/she/it did speak - **habló**

PLUR. We spoke *or* we did speak - **hablamos**
You spoke *or* you did speak - **hablasteis** (fam.), - **Ustedes hablaron** (form.)
They spoke *or* they did speak - **hablaron**

Past (Indefinite)

SING. I have spoken - **he hablado**
You have spoken - **has habado** (fam.), - **Usted ha hablado** (form.)
He/she/it has spoken - **ha hablado**

PLUR. We have spoken - **hemos hablado**
You have spoken - **habéis hablado** (fam.), - **Ustedes han hablado** (form.)
They have spoken - **han hablado**

Past (Imperfect *or* Continuous)

SING. I was speaking *or* I used to speak - **hablaba**
You were speaking or you used to speak - **hablabas** (fam.), - **Usted hablaba** (form.)
He/she/it was speaking *or* he/she/it used to speak - **hablaba**

PLUR. We were speaking *or* we used to speak - **hablábamos**
You were speaking *or* you used to speak - **hablabais** (fam.), - **Ustedes hablaban** (form.)
They were speaking *or* they used to speak - **hablaban**

Gerund

Speaking - **hablando**

To Stay or Remain - **Permanecer**

(Per-man-eth-air)

Not to be confused with To Stop Over - **Parar**

Present

SING. I stay, I do stay *or* I am staying - **permanezco**
You stay, you do stay *or* you are staying - **permanceces** (fam.), - **Usted permanece** (form.)
He/she/it stays, he/she/it does stay *or* he/she/it is staying - **permanece**

PLUR. We stay, we do stay, *or* we are staying - **permanecemos**
You stay, you do stay, *or* you are staying - **permanecéis** (fam.), - **Ustedes permanecen** (form.)
They stay, they do stay *or* they are staying - **permanecen**

Future

SING. I shall stay - **permaneceré**
You will stay - **permanecerás** (fam.), - **Usted permanecerá** (form.)
He/she/it will stay - **permanecerá**

PLUR. We shall stay - **permaneceremos**
You will stay - **permaneceréis** (fam.), - **Ustedes permanecerán** (form.)
They will stay - **permanecerán**

Past (Preterit)

SING. I stayed *or* I did stay - **permanecí**
You stayed *or* you did stay - **permaneciste** (fam.), - **Usted permaneció** (form.)
He/she/it stayed *or* he/she/it did stay - **permaneció**

PLUR. We stayed *or* we did stay - **permanecimos**
You stayed *or* you did stay - **permanecisteis** (fam.), - **Ustedes permanecieron** (form.)
They stayed *or* they did stay - **permanecieron**

Past (Indefinite)

SING. I have stayed - **he permanecido**
You have stayed - **has permanecido** (fam.), - **Usted ha permanecido** (form.)
He/she/it has stayed - **ha permanecido**

PLUR. We have stayed - **hemos permanecido**
You have stayed - **habéis permanecido** (fam.), - **Ustedes han permanecido** (form.)
They have stayed - **han permanecido**

Past (Imperfect *or* Continuous)

SING. I was staying *or* I used to stay - **permanecía**
You were staying *or* you used to stay - **permanecías** (fam.), - **Usted permanecía** (form.)
He/she/it was staying *or* he/she/it used to stay - **permanecía**

PLUR. We were staying *or* we used to stay - **permanecíamos**
You were staying *or* you used to stay - **permanecíais** (fam.), - **Ustedes permanecían** (form.)
They were staying *or* they used to stay - **permanecían**

Gerund

Staying *or* Remaining - **permaneciendo**

To Stay *or* Stop Over - **Parar** (As in a hotel)

Present

SING. I stay, I do stay *or* I am staying - **paro**
You stay, you do stay *or* you are staying - **paras** (fam.), - **Usted para** (form.)
He/she/it stays, he/she/it does stay *or* he/she/it is staying - **para**

PLUR. We stay, we do stay *or* we are staying - **paramos**
You stay, you do stay *or* you are staying - **paráis** (fam.), - **Ustedes paran** (form.)
They stay, they do stay *or* they are staying - **paran**

Future

SING. I shall stay - **pararé**
You will stay - **pararás** (fam.), - **Usted parará** (form.)
He/she/it will stay - **parará**

PLUR. We shall stay - **pararemos**
You will stay - **pararéis** (fam.), - **Ustedes pararán** (form.)
They will stay - **pararán**

Past (Preterit)

SING. I stayed *or* I did stay - **paré**
You stayed *or* you did stay - **paraste** (fam), - **Usted paró** (form.)
He/she/it stayed *or* he/she/it did stay - **paró**

PLUR.We stayed *or* we did stay - **paramos**
You stayed *or* you did stay - **parasteis** (fam.), - **Ustedes pararon** (form.)
They stayed *or* they did stay - **pararon**

Past (Indefinite)

SING. I have stayed - **he parado**
You have stayed - **has parado** (fam.) - **Usted ha parado** (form.)
He/she/it has stayed - **ha parado**

PLUR. We have stayed - **hemos parado**
You have stayed - **habéis parado** (fam.), - **Ustedes han parado** (form.)
They have stayed - **han parado**

Past (Imperfect *or* Continuous)

SING. I was staying *or* I used to stay - **paraba**
You were staying *or* you used to stay - **parabas** (fam.), - **Usted paraba** (form.)
He/she/it was staying *or* he/she/it used to stay - **paraba**

PLUR. We were staying *or* we used to stay - **parábamos**
You were staying *or* you used to stay - **parabais** (fam.), - **Ustedes paraban** (form.)
They were staying *or* they used to stay - **paraban**

Gerund

Staying *or* Stopping Over - **parando**

To Suppose - **Suponer**
(*Soo-pon-air*)

Present

SING. I suppose, I do suppose *or* I am supposing - **supongo**
You suppose, you do suppose *or* you are supposing - **supones** (fam.), - **Usted supone** (form.)
He/she supposes, he/she does suppose *or* he/she is supposing - **supone**

PLUR. We suppose, we do suppose *or* we are supposing - **suponemos**
You suppose, you do suppose *or* you are supposing - **suponéis** (fam.), - **Ustedes suponen** (form.)
They suppose, they do suppose *or* they are supposing - **suponen**

Future

SING. I shall suppose - **supondré**
You will suppose - **supondrás** (fam.), - **Usted supondrá** (form.)
He/she will suppose - **supondrá**

PLUR. We shall suppose - **supondremos**
You will suppose - **supondréis** (fam.), - **Ustedes supondrán** (form.)
They will suppose - **supondrán**

Past (Preterit)

SING. I supposed *or* I did suppose - **supuse**
You supposed *or* you did suppose - **supusiste** (fam.), - **Usted supuso** (form.)
He/she supposed *or* he/she did suppose - **supuso**

PLUR. We supposed *or* we did suppose - **supusimos**
You supposed *or* you did suppose - **supusisteis** (fam.), - **Ustedes supusieron** (form.)
They supposed *or* they did suppose - **supusieron**

Past (Indefinite)

SING. I have supposed - **he supuesto**
You have supposed - **has supuesto** (fam.), - **Usted ha supuesto** (form.)
He/she has supposed - **ha supuesto**

PLUR. We have supposed - **hemos supuesto**
You have supposed - **habeis supuesto** (fam.), - **Ustedes han supuesto** (form.)
They have supposed - **han supuesto**

Past (Imperfect *or* Continuous)

SING. I was supposing *or* I used to suppose - **suponía**
You were supposing *or* you used to suppose - **suponías** (fam.), - **Usted suponía** (form.)
He/she was supposing *or* he/she used to suppose - **suponía**

PLUR. We were supposing *or* we used to suppose - **suponíamos**
You were supposing *or* you used to suppose - **suponíais** (fam.), - **Ustedes suponían** (form.)
They were supposing *or* they used to suppose - **suponían**

Gerund

Supposing - **suponiendo**

To Take - **Tomar**
(Also used in relation to "having" something to eat or drink)

Present

SING. I take, I do take *or* I am taking - **tomo**
You take, you do take *or* you are taking - **tomas** (fam.), - **Usted toma** (form.)
He/she/it takes, he/she/it does take *or* he/she/it is taking - **toma**

PLUR. We take, we do take *or* we are taking - **tomamos**
You take, you do take *or* you are taking - **tomáis** (fam.), - **Ustedes toman** (form.)
They take, they do take *or* they are taking - **toman**

Future

SING. I shall take - **tomaré**
You will take - **tomarás** (fam.), - **Usted tomará** (form.)
He/she/it will take - **tomará**

PLUR. We shall take - **tomaremos**
You will take - **tomaréis** (fam.), - **Ustedes tomarán** (form.)
They will take - **tomarán**

Past (Preterit)

SING. I took *or* I did take - **tomé**
You took *or* you did take - **tomaste** (fam.), - **Usted tomó** (form.)
He/she/it took *or* he/she/it did take - **tomó**

PLUR. We took *or* we did take - **tomamos**
You took *or* you did take - **tomasteis** (fam.), - **Ustedes tomaron** (form.)
They took *or* they did take - **tomaron**

Past (Indefinite)

SING. I have taken - **he tomado**
You have taken - **has tomado** (fam.), - **Usted ha tomado** (form.)
He/she/it has taken - **ha tomado**

PLUR. We have taken - **hemos tomado**
You have taken - **habéis tomado** (fam.), - **Ustedes han tomado** (form.)
They have taken - **han tomado**

Past (Imperfect *or* Continuous)

SING. I was taking *or* I used to take - **tomaba**
You were taking *or* you used to take - **tomabas** (fam.), - **Usted tomaba** (form.)
He/she/it was taking *or* he/she/it used to take - **tomaba**

PLUR. We were taking *or* we used to take - **tomábamos**
You were taking *or* you used to take - **tomabais** (fam.), - **Ustedes tomaban** (form.)
They were taking *or* they used to take - **tomaban**

Gerund

Taking - **tomando**

To Take Out *or* Get Something Out - **Sacar**

Present

SING. I take out, I do take out *or* I am taking out - **saco**
You take out, you do take out *or* you are taking out - **sacas** (fam.), - **Usted saca** (form.)
He/she/it takes out, he/she/it does take out *or* he/she/it is taking out - **saca**

PLUR. We take out, we do take out *or* we are taking out - **sacamos**
You take out, you do take out *or* you are taking out - **sacáis** (fam.), - **Ustedes sacan** (form.)
They take out, they do take out *or* they are taking out - **sacan**

Future

SING. I shall take out - **sacaré**
You will take out - **sacarás** (fam.), - **Usted sacará** (form.)
He/she/it will take out - **sacará**

PLUR. We shall take out - **sacaremos**
You will take out - **sacaréis** (fam.), - **Ustedes sacarán** (form.)
They will take out - **sacarán**

Past (Preterit)

SING. I took out *or* I did take out - **saqué**
You took out *or* you did take out - **sacaste** (fam.), - **Usted sacó** (form.)
He/she/it took out *or* he/she/it did take out - **sacó**

PLUR. We took out *or* we did take out - **sacamos**
You took out *or* you did take out - **sacasteis** (fam.), - **Ustedes sacaron** (form.)
They took out *or* they did take out - **sacaron**

Past (Indefinite)

SING. I have taken out - **he sacado**
You have taken out - **has sacado** (fam.), - **Usted ha sacado** (form.)
He/she/it has taken out - **ha sacado**

PLUR. We have taken out - **hemos sacado**
You have taken out - **habéis sacado** (fam.), - **Ustedes han sacado** (form.)
They have taken out - **han sacado**

Past (Imperfect *or* Continuous)

SING. I was taking out *or* I used to take out - **sacaba**
You were taking out *or* you used to take out - **sacabas** (fam.), - **Usted sacaba** (form.)
He/she/it was taking out *or* he/she/it used to take out - **sacaba**

PLUR. We were taking out *or* we used to take out - **sacábamos**
You were taking out *or* you used to take out - **sacabais** (fam.), - **Ustedes sacaban** (form.)
They were taking out *or* they used to take out - **sacaban**

Gerund

Taking out - **sacando**

To Taste *or* To Try - **Probar**
Also To Test

Present

SING. I taste, I do taste *or* I am tasting - **pruebo**
You taste, you do taste *or* you are tasting - **pruebas** (fam.), - **Usted prueba** (form.)
He/she/it tastes, he/she/it does taste *or* he/she/it is tasting - **prueba**

PLUR. We taste, we do taste *or* we are tasting - **probamos**
You taste, you do taste *or* you are tasting - **probáis** (fam.), - **Ustedes prueban** (form.)
They taste, they do taste *or* they are tasting - **prueban**

Future

SING. I shall taste - **probaré**
You will taste - **probarás** (fam.), - **Usted probará** (form.)
He/she/it will taste - **probará**

PLUR. We shall taste - **probaremos**
You will taste - **probaréis** (fam.), - **Ustedes probarán** (form.)
They will taste - **probarán**

Past (Preterit)

SING. I tasted *or* I did taste - **probé**
You tasted *or* you did taste - **probaste** (fam.), - **Usted probó** (form.)
He/she/it tasted *or* he/she/it did taste - **probó**

PLUR. We tasted *or* we did taste - **probamos**
You tasted *or* you did taste - **probasteis** (fam.), - **Ustedes probaron** (form.)
They tasted *or* they did taste - **probaron**

Past (Indefinite)

SING. I have tasted - **he probado**
You have tasted - **has probado** (fam.), - **Usted ha probado** (form.)
He/she/it has tasted - **ha probado**

PLUR. We have tasted - **hemos probado**
You have tasted - **habéis probado** (fam.), - **Ustedes han probado** (form.)
They have tasted - **han probado**

Past (Imperfect *or* Continuous)

SING. I was tasting *or* I used to taste - **probaba**
You were tasting *or* you used to taste- **probabas** (fam.), - **Usted probaba** (form.)
He/she/it was tasting *or* he/she/it used to taste - **probaba**

PLUR. We were tasting *or* we used to taste - **probábamos**
You were tasting *or* you used to taste - **probabais** (fam.), - **Ustedes probaban** (form..)
They were tasting *or* they used to taste - **probaban**

Gerund

Tasting, testing *or* trying - **probando**

To Teach - **Enseñar**
(*En-sen-yar*)

Present

SING. I teach, I do teach *or* I am teaching - **enseño**
You teach, you do teach *or* you are teaching - **enseñas** (fam.), - **Usted enseña** (form.)
He/she/it teaches, he/she/it does teach *or* he/she/it is teaching - **enseña**

PLUR. We teach, we do teach *or* we are teaching - **enseñamos**
You teach, you do teach *or* you are teaching - **enseñáis** (fam.), - **Ustedes enseñan** (form.)
They teach, they do teach *or* they are teaching - **enseñan**

Future

SING. I shall teach - **enseñaré**
You will teach - **enseñaràs** (fam.), - **Usted enseñará** (form.)
He/she/it will teach - **enseñará**

PLUR. We shall teach - **enseñaremos**
You will teach - **enseñaréis** (fam.), - **Ustedes enseñarán** (form.)
They will teach - **enseñarán**

Past (Preterit)

SING. I taught *or* I did teach - **enseñé**
You taught *or* you did teach - **enseñaste** (fam.), - **Usted enseñó** (form.)
He/she/it taught *or* he/she/it did teach - **enseñó**

PLUR. We taught *or* we did teach - **enseñamos**
You taught *or* you did teach - **enseñasteis** (fam.), - **Ustedes enseñaron** (form.)
They taught *or* they did teach - **enseñaron**

Past (Indefinite)

SING. I have taught - **he enseñado**
You have taught - **has enseñado** (fam.), - **Usted ha enseñado** (form.)
He/she/it has taught - **ha enseñado**

PLUR. We have taught - **hemos enseñado**
You have taught - **habéis enseñado** (fam.), - **Ustedes han enseñado** (form.)
They have taught - **han enseñado**

Past (Imperfect *or* Continuous)

SING. I was teaching *or* I used to teach - **enseñaba**
You were teaching *or* you used to teach - **enseñabas (fam.)**, - **Usted enseñaba** (form.)
He/she/it was teaching *or* he/she/it used to teach - **enseñaba**

PLUR. We were teaching *or* we used to teach - **enseñábamos**
You were teaching *or* you used to teach - **enseñabais** (fam.), - **Ustedes enseñaban** (form.)
They were teaching *or* they used to teach - **enseñaban**

Gerund

Teaching - **enseñando**

To Think - **Pensar**
(Not to be confused with To Believe - **Creer**)

Present

SING. I think, I do think *or* I am thinking - **pienso**
You think, you do think *or* you are thinking - **piensas** (fam.), - **Usted piensa** (form.)
He/she/it thinks, he/she/it does think *or* he/she/it is thinking - **piensa**

PLUR. We think, we do think *or* we are thinking - **pensamos**
You think, you do think *or* you are thinking - **pensáis** (fam.), - **Ustedes piensan** (form.)
They think, they do think *or* they are thinking - **piensan**

Future

SING. I shall think - **pensaré**
You will think - **pensarás** (fam.), - **Usted pensará** (form.)
He/she/it will think - **pensará**

PLUR. We shall think - **pensaremos**
You will think - **pensaréis** (fam.), - **Ustedes pensarán** (form.)
They will think - **pensarán**

Past (Preterit)

SING. I thought *or* I did think - **pensé**
You thought *or* you did think - **pensaste** (fam.), - **Usted pensó** (form.)
He/she/it thought *or* he/she/it did think - **pensó**

PLUR. We thought *or* we did think - **pensamos**
You thought *or* you did think - **pensasteis** (fam.), - **Ustedes pensaron** (form.)
They thought *or* they did think - **pensaron**

Past (Indefinite)

SING. I have thought - **he pensado**
You have thought - **has pensado** (fam), - **Usted ha pensado** (form.)
He/she/it has thought - **ha pensado**

PLUR. We have thought - **hemos pensado**
You have thought - **habéis pensado** (fam.), - **Ustedes han pensado** (form.)
They have thought - **han pensado**

Past (Imperfect *or* Continuous)

SING. I was thinking *or* I used to think - **pensaba**
You were thinking *or* you used to think - **pensabas** (fam.), - **Usted pensaba** (form.)
He/she/it was thinking *or* he/she/it used to think **pensaba**

PLUR. We were thinking *or* we used to think - **pensábamos**
You were thinking *or* you used to think - **pensabais** (fam.), - **Ustedes pensaban** (form.)
They were thinking *or* they used to think - **pensaban**

Gerund

Thinking - **pensando**

To Touch - **Tocar**
(*Tock-ar*)
(Also To Play a musical instrument)

Present

SING. I touch, I do touch *or* I am touching - **yo toco**
You touch, you do touch *or* you are touching - **tú tocas** (fam.), - **Usted toca** (form.)
He/she/it touches, he/she/it does touch *or* he/she/it is touching - **toca**

PLUR. We touch, we do touch *or* we are touching - **tocamos**
You touch, you do touch *or* you are touching - **tocáis** (fam.), - **Ustedes tocan** (form.)
They touch, they do touch *or* they are touching - **tocan**

Future

SING. I shall touch - **tocaré**
You will touch - **tocarás** (fam.), - **Usted tocará** (form.)
He/she/it will touch - **tocará**

PLUR. We shall touch - **tocaremos**
You will touch - **tocaréis** (fam.), - **Ustedes tocarán** (form.)
They will touch - **tocarán**

Past (Preterit)

SING. I touched *or* I did touch - **toqué**
You touched *or* you did touch - **tocaste** (fam.), - **Usted tocó** (form.)
He/she/it touched *or* he/she/it did touch - **tocó**

PLUR. We touched *or* we did touch - **tocamos**
You touched *or* you did touch - **tocasteis** (fam.), - **Ustedes tocaron** (form.)
They touched *or* they did touch - **tocaron**

Past (Indefinite)

SING. I have touched - **he tocado**
You have touched - **has tocado** (fam.), - **Usted ha tocado** (form.)
He/she/it has touched - **ha tocado**

PLUR. We have touched - **hemos tocado**
You have touched - **habéis tocado** (fam.), - **Ustedes han tocado** (form.)
They have touched - **han tocado**

Past (Imperfect *or* Continuous)

SING. I was touching *or* I used to touch - **tocaba**
You were touching *or* you used to touch - **tocabas** (fam.), - **Usted tocaba** (form.)
He/she/it was touching *or* he/she/it used to touch - **tocaba**

PLUR. We were touching *or* we used to touch - **tocábamos**
You were touching *or* you used to touch - **tocabais** (fam.), - **Ustedes tocaban** (form.)
They were touching *or* they used to touch - **tocaban**

Gerund

Touching *or* Playing a musical instrument - **tocando**

To Translate - **Traducir**
(*Trad-oo-theer*)

Present

SING. I translate, I do translate *or* I am translating - **yo traduzco**
You translate, you do translate *or* you are translating - **tú traduces** (fam.), - **Usted traduce** (form.)
He/she/it translates, he/she/it does translate *or* he/she/it is translating - **traduce**

PLUR. We translate, we do translate *or* we are translating - **traducimos**
You translate, you do translate *or* you are translating - **traducís** (fam.), - **Ustedes traducen** (form.)
They translate, they do translate *or* they are translating - **traducen**

Future

SING. I shall translate - **traduciré**
You will translate - **traducirás** (fam.), - **Usted traducirá** (form.)
He/she/it will translate - **traducirá**

PLUR. We shall translate - **traduciremos**
You will translate - **traduciréis** (fam.), - **Ustedes traducirán** (form.)
They will translate - **traducirán**

Past (Preterit)

SING. I translated *or* I did translate - **traduje**
You translated *or* you did translate - **tradujiste** (fam.), - **Usted tradujo** (form.)
He/she/it translated *or* he/she/it did translate - **tradujo**

PLUR. We translated *or* we did translate - **tradujimos**
You translated *or* you did translate - **tradujisteis** (fam.), - **Ustedes tradujeron** (form.)
They translated *or* they did translate - **tradujeron**

Past (Indefinite)

SING. I have translated - **he traducido**
You have translated - **has traducido** (fam.), - **Usted ha traducido** (form.)
He/she/it has translated - **ha traducido**

PLUR. We have translated - **hemos traducido**
You have translated - **habéis traducido** (fam.), - **Ustedes han traducido** (form.)
They have translated - **han traducido**

Past (Imperfect *or* Continuous)

SING. I was translating *or* I used to translate - **traducía**
You were translating *or* you used to translate - **traducías** (fam.), - **Usted traducía** (form.)
He/she/it was translating *or* he/she/it used to translate - **traducía**

PLUR. We were translating *or* we used to translate - **traducíamos**
You were translating *or* you used to translate - **traducíais** (fam.), - **Ustedes traducían** (form.)
They were translating *or* they used to translate - **traducían**

Gerund

Translating - **traduciendo**

To Travel - **Viajar**
(*Vee-aa-kar*)

Present

SING. I travel, I do travel *or* I am travelling - **viajo**
You travel, you do travel *or* you are travelling - **viajas** (fam.), **Usted viaja** (form.)
He/she/it travels, he/she/it does travel *or* he/she/it is travelling - **viaja**

PLUR. We travel, we do travel *or* we are travelling - **viajamos**
You travel, you do travel *or* you are travelling - **viajáis** (fam.), - **Ustedes viajan** (form.)
They travel, they do travel *or* they are travelling - **viajan**

Future

SING. I shall travel - **viajaré**
You will travel - **viajarás** (fam.), - **Usted viajará** (form.)
He/she/it will travel - **viajará**

PLUR. We shall travel - **viajaremos**
You will travel - **viajaréis** (fam.), - **Ustedes viajarán** (form.)
They will travel - **viajarán**

Past (Preterit)

SING. I travelled *or* I did travel - **viajé**
You travelled *or* you did travel - **viajaste** (fam.), **Usted viajó** (form.)
He/she/it travelled *or* he/she/it did travel - **viajó**

PLUR. We travelled *or* we did travel - **viajamos**
You travelled *or* you did travel - **viajasteis** (fam.), - **Ustedes viajaron** (form.)
They travelled *or* they did travel - **viajaron**

Past (Indefinite)

SING. I have travelled - **he viajado**
You have travelled - **has viajado** (fam.), - **Usted ha viajado** (form.)
He/she/it has travelled - **ha viajado**

PLUR. We have travelled - **hemos viajado**
You have travelled - **habéis viajado** (fam.), - **Ustedes han viajado** (form.)
They have travelled - **han viajado**

Past (Imperfect *or* Continuous)

SING. I was travelling *or* I used to travel - **viajaba**
You were travelling *or* you used to travel - **viajabas** (fam.), **Usted viajaba** (form.)
He/she/it was travelling *or* he/she/it used to travel - **viajaba**

PLUR. We were travelling *or* we used to travel - **viajábamos**
You were travelling *or* you used to travel - **viajabais** (fam.), - **Ustedes viajaban** (form.)
They were travelling *or* they used to travel - **viajaban**

Gerund

Travelling - **viajando**

To Try *or* To Attempt - **Intentar** (Not to be confused with To Taste - **Probar**)

Present

SING. I try, I do try *or* I am trying - **intento**
You try, you do try *or* you are trying - **intentas** (fam.), - **Usted intenta** (form.)
He/she/it tries, he/she/it does try *or* he/she/it is trying - **intenta**

PLUR. We try, we do try *or* we are trying - **intentamos**
You try, you do try *or* you are trying - **intentáis** (fam.), - **Ustedes intentan** (form.)
They try, they do try *or* they are trying - **intentan**

Future

SING. I shall try - **intentaré**
You will try - **intentarás** (fam.), - **Usted intentará** (form.)
He/she/it will try - **intentará**

PLUR. We shall try - **intentaremos**
You will try - **intentaréis** (fam.), - **Ustedes intentarán** (form.)
They will try - **intentarán**

Past (Preterit)

SING. I tried *or* I did try - **intenté**
You tried *or* you did try - **intentaste** (fam.), - **Usted intentó** (form.)
He/she/it tried *or* he/she/it did try - **intentó**

PLUR. We tried *or* we did try - **intentamos**
You tried *or* you did try - **intentasteis** (fam.), - **Ustedes intentaron** (form.)
They tried *or* they did try - **intentaron**

Past (Indefinite)

SING. I have tried - **he intentado**
You have tried - **has intentado** (fam.), - **Usted ha intentado** (form.)
He/she/it has tried - **ha intentado**

PLUR. We have tried - **hemos intentado**
You have tried - **habéis intentado** (fam.), - **Ustedes han intentado** (form.)
They have tried - **han intentado**

Past (Imperfect *or* Continuous)

SING. I was trying *or* I used to try - **intentaba**
You were tryinng *or* you used to try - **intentabas** (fam.), - **Usted intentaba** (form.)
He/she/it was trying *or* he/she/it used to try - **intentaba**

PLUR. We were trying *or* we used to try - **intentábamos**
You were trying *or* you used to try - **intentabais** (fam.), - **Ustedes intentaban** (form.)
They were trying *or* they used to try - **intentaban**

Gerund

Trying - **intentando**

To Understand - Entender
(*En-ten-dair*)

(Also **Comprender**, but **Entender** seems to be more commonly used)

Present

SING. I understand, I do understand *or* I am understanding - **entiendo**
You understand, you do understand *or* you are understanding - **entiendes** (fam.), - **Usted entiende** (form.)
He/she/it understands, he/she/it does understand *or* he/she/it is understanding - **entiende**

PLUR. We understand, we do understand *or* we are understanding - **entendemos**
You understand, you do understand *or* you are understanding - **entendéis** (fam.), - **Ustedes entienden** (form.)
They understand, they do understand *or* they are understanding - **entienden**

Future

SING. I shall understand - **entenderé**
You will understand - **entenderás** (fam.), - **Usted entenderá** (form.)
He/she/it will understand - **entenderá**

PLUR. We shall understand - **entenderemos**
You will understand - **entenderéis** (fam.), - **Ustedes entenderán** (form.)
They will understand - **entenderán**

Past (Preterit)

SING. I understood *or* I did understand - **entendí**
You understood *or* you did understand - **entendiste** (fam.), - **Usted entendió** (form.)
He/she/it understood *or* he/she/it did understand - **entendió**

PLUR. We understood *or* we did understand - **entendimos**
You understood *or* you did understand - **entendisteis** (fam.), - **Ustedes entendieron** (form.)
They understood *or* they did understand - **entendieron**

Past (Indefinite)

SING. I have understood - **he entendido**
You have understood - **has entendido** (fam.), - **Usted ha entendido** (form.)
He/she/it has understood - **ha entendido**

PLUR. We have understood - **hemos entendido**
You have understood **habéis entendido** (fam.), - **Ustedes han entendido** (form.)
They have understood - **han entendido**

Past (Imperfect *or* Continuous)

SING. I was understanding *or* I used to understand - **entendía**
You were understanding *or* you used to understand - **entendías** (fam.), - **Usted entendía** (form.)
He/she/it was understanding *or* he/she/it used to understand - **entendía**

PLUR. We were understanding *or* we used to understand -**entendíamos**
You were understanding *or* you used to understand - **entendíais** (fam.), - **Ustedes entendían** (form.)
They were understanding *or* they used to understand - **entendían**

Gerund

Understanding - **entendiendo**

To Use - **Usar**
(Oo-sar)

Also **Emplear**

Present

SING. I use, I do use *or* I am using - **uso**
You use, you do use *or* you are using - **usas** (fam.), - **Usted usa** (form.)
He/she/it uses, he/she/it does use *or* he/she/it is using - **usa**

PLUR. We use, we do use *or* we are using - **usamos**
You use, you do use *or* you are using - **usáis** (fam.), - **Ustedes usan** (form.)
They use, they do use *or* they are using - **usan**

Future

SING. I shall use - **usaré**
You will use - **usarás** (fam.), - **Usted usará** (form.)
He/she/it will use - **usará**

PLUR. We shall use - **usaremos**
You will use - **usaréis** (fam.), - **Ustedes usarán** (form.)
They will use - **usarán**

Past (Preterit)

SING. I used *or* I did use - **usé**
You used *or* you did use - **usaste** (fam.), - **Usted usó** (form.)
He/she/it used *or* he/she/it did use - **usó**

PLUR. We used *or* we did use - **usamos**
You used *or* you did use - **usasteis** (fam.), - **Ustedes usaron** (form.)
They used *or* they did use - **usaron**

Past (Indefinite)

SING. I have used - **he usado**
You have used - **has usado** (fam.), - **Usted ha usado** (form.)
He/she/it has used - **ha usado**

PLUR. We have used - **hemos usado**
You have used - **habéis usado** (fam.), - **Ustedes han usado** (form.)
They have used - **han usado**

Past (Imperfect *or* Continuous)

SING. I was using *or* I used to use - **usaba**
You were using *or* you used to use - **usabas** (fam.), - **Usted usaba** (form.)
He/she/it was using *or* he/she/it used to use - **usaba**

PLUR. We were using *or* we used to use - **usábamos**
You were using *or* you used to use - **usabais** (fam.), - **Ustedes usaban** (form.)
They were using *or* they used to use - **usaban**

Gerund

Using - **usando**

To Wait - **Esperar**
(Also To Hope and To Expect)

Present

SING. I wait, I do wait *or* I am waiting - **espero**
You wait, you do wait *or* you are waiting - **esperas** (fam.), - **Usted espera** (form.)
He/she/it waits, he/she/it does wait *or* he/she/it is waiting - **espera**

PLUR. We wait, we do wait *or* we are waiting - **esperamos**
You wait, you do wait *or* you are waiting - **esperáis** (fam.), - **Ustedes esperan** (form.)
They wait, they do wait *or* they are waiting - **esperan**

Future

SING. I shall wait - **esperaré**
You will wait - **esperarás** (fam.), - **Usted esperará** (form.)
He/she/it will wait - **esperará**

PLUR. We shall wait - **esperaremos**
You will wait - **esperaréis** (fam.), - **Ustedes esperarán** (form.)
They will wait - **esperarán**

Past (Preterit)

SING. I waited *or* I did wait - **esperé**
You waited *or* you did wait - **esperaste** (fam.), - **Usted esperó** (form.)
He/she/it waited *or* he/she/it did wait - **esperó**

PLUR. We waited *or* we did wait - **esperamos**
You waited *or* you did wait - **esperasteis** (fam.), - **Ustedes esperaron** (form.)
They waited *or* they did wait - **esperaron**

Past (Indefinite)

SING. I have waited - **he esperado**
You have waited - **has esperado** (fam.), - **Usted ha esperado** (form.)
He/she/it has waited - **ha esperado**

PLUR. We have waited - **hemos esperado**
You have waited - **habéis esperado** (fam.), - **Ustedes han esperado** (form.)
They have waited - **han esperado**

Past (Imperfect *or* Continuous)

SING. I was waiting *or* I used to wait - **esperaba**
You were waiting *or* you used to wait - **esperabas** (fam.), - **Usted esperaba** (form.)
He/she/it was waiting *or* he/she/it used to wait - **esperaba**

PLUR. We were waiting *or* we used to wait - **esperábamos**
You were waiting *or* you used to wait - **esperabais** (fam.), - **Ustedes esperaban** (form.)
They were waiting *or* they used to wait - **esperaban**

Gerund

Waiting, Hoping *or* Expecting - **esperando**

To Walk - **Andar**

Present

SING. I walk, I do walk *or* I am walking - **yo ando**
You walk, you do walk *or* you are walking - **tú andas** (fam.), - **Usted anda** (form.)
He/she/it walks, he/she/it does walk *or* he/she/it is walking - **anda**

PLUR. We walk, we do walk *or* we are walking - **andamos**
You walk, you do walk *or* you are walking - **andáis** (fam.), - **Ustedes andan** (form.)
They walk, they do walk *or* they are walking - **andan**

Future

SING. I shall walk - **andaré**
You will walk - **andarás** (fam.), - **Usted andará** (form.)
He/she/it will walk - **andará**

PLUR. We shall walk - **andaremos**
You will walk - **andaréis** (fam.) - **Ustedes andarán** (form.)
They will walk - **andarán**

Past (Preterit)

SING. I walked *or* I did walk - **anduve**
You walked *or* you did walk - **anduviste** (fam.), - **Usted anduvo** (form.)
He/she/it walked *or* he/she/it did walk - **anduvo**

PLUR. We walked *or* we did walk - **anduvimos**
You walked *or* you did walk - **anduvisteis** (fam.), - **Ustedes anduvieron** (form.)
They walked *or* they did walk - **anduvieron**

Past (Indefinite)

SING. I have walked - **he andado**
You have walked - **has andado** (fam.), - **Usted ha andado** (form.)
He/she/it has walked - **ha andado**

PLUR. We have walked - **hemos andado**
You have walked - **habéis andado** (fam.), - **Ustedes han andado** (form.)
They have walked - **han andado**

Past (Imperfect *or* Continuous)

SING. I was walking *or* I used to walk - **andaba**
You were walking *or* you used to walk - **andabas** (fam.), - **Usted andaba** (form.)
He/she/it was walking *or* he/she/it used to walk - **andaba**

PLUR. We were walking *or* we used to walk - **andábamos**
You were walking *or* you used to walk - **andabais** (fam.), - **Ustedes andaban** (form.)
They were walking *or* they used to walk- **andaban**

Gerund

Walking - **andando**

To Want - **Querer**
(*Care-air*)
(Also To Wish, use also for "Would Like")

Present

SING. I want, I do want *or* I am wanting - **quiero**
You want, you do want *or* you are wanting - **quieres** (fam.), - **Usted quiere** (form.)
He/she/it wants, he/she/it does want *or* he/she/it is wanting - **quiere**

PLUR. We want, we do want *or* we are wanting - **queremos**
You want, you do want *or* you are wanting - **queréis** (fam.), - **Ustedes quieren** (form.)
They want, they do want *or* they are wanting - **quieren**

Future

SING. I shall want - **querré**
You will want - **querrás** (fam.), - **Usted querrá** (form.)
He/she/it will want - **querrá**

PLUR. We shall want - **querremos**
You will want - **querréis** (fam.), - **Ustedes querrán** (form.)
They will want - **querrán**

Past (Preterit)

SING. I wanted *or* I did want - **quise**
You wanted *or* you did want - **quisiste** (fam.), - **Usted quiso** (form.)
He/she/it wanted *or* he/she/it did want - **quiso**

PLUR. We wanted *or* we did want - **quisimos**
You wanted *or* you did want - **quisisteis** (fam.), - **Ustedes quisieron** (form.)
They wanted *or* they did want - **quisieron**

Past (Indefinite)

SING. I have wanted - **he querido**
You have wanted - **has querido** (fam.), - **Usted ha querido** (form.)
He/she/it has wanted - **ha querido**

PLUR. We have wanted - **hemos querido**
You have wanted - **habéis querido** (fam.), - **Ustedes han querido** (form.)
They have wanted - **han querido**

Past (Imperfect *or* Continuous)

SING. I was wanting *or* I used to want - **quería**
You were wanting *or* you used to want - **querías** (fam.), - **Usted quería** (form.)
He/she/it was wanting *or* he/she/it used to want - **quería**

PLUR. We were wanting *or* we used to want - **queríamos**
You were wanting *or* you used to want - **queríais** (fam.), - **Ustedes querían** (form.)
They were wanting *or* they used to want - **querían**

Gerund

Wanting - **queriendo**

To Wash - **Lavar**

Present

SING. I wash, I do wash *or* I am washing - **lavo**
You wash, you do wash *or* you are washing - **lavas** (fam.), - **Usted lava** (form.)
He/she/it washes, he/she/it does wash *or* he/she/it is washing - **lava**

PLUR. We wash, we do wash *or* we are washing - **lavamos**
You wash, you do wash *or* you are washing - **laváis** (fam.) - **Ustedes lavan** (form.)
They wash, they do wash *or* they are washing - **lavan**

Future

SING. I shall wash - **lavaré**
You will wash - **lavarás** (fam.), - **Usted lavará** (form.)
He/she/it will wash - **lavará**

PLUR. We shall wash - **lavaremos**
You will wash - **lavaréis** (fam.), - **Ustedes lavarán** (form.)
They will wash - **lavarán**

Past (Preterit)

SING. I washed *or* I did wash - **lavé**
You washed *or* you did wash - **lavaste** (fam.), - **Usted lavó** (form.)
He/she/it washed *or* he/she/it did wash - **lavó**

PLUR. We washed *or* we did wash - **lavamos**
You washed *or* you did wash - **lavasteis** (fam.), - **Ustedes lavaron** (form.)
They washed *or* they did wash - **lavaron**

Past (Indefinite)

SING.I have washed - **he lavado**
You have washed - **has lavado** (fam.), - **Usted ha lavado** (form.)
He/she/it has washed - **ha lavado**

PLUR.We have washed - **hemos lavado**
You have washed - **habéis lavado** (form.), - **Ustedes han lavado** (form.)
They have washed - **han lavado**

Past (Imperfect or Continuous)

SING.I was washing *or* I used to wash - **lavaba**
You were washing *or* you used to wash - **lavabas** (fam.), - **Usted lavaba** (form.)
He/she/it was washing *or* he/she/it used to wash - **lavaba**

PLUR.We were washing *or* we used to wash - **lavábamos**
You were washing *or* you used to wash - **lavabais** (fam.), - **Ustedes lavaban** (form.)
They were washing *or* they used to wash - **lavaban**

Gerund

Washing - **lavando**

To Wash Oneself - **Lavarse**
(Lav-ar-say)

Present

SING. I wash myself, I do wash myself *or* I am washing myself - **me lavo**
You wash yourself, you do wash yourself *or* you are washing yourself - **te lavas** (fam.), - **Usted se lava** (form.)
He/she/it washes him/her/itself, he/she/it does wash him/her/itself *or* he/she/it is washing him/her/itself - **se lava**

PLUR. We wash ourselves, we do wash ourselves *or* we are washing ourselves - **nos lavamos**
You wash yourselves, you do wash yourselves *or* you are washing yourselves - **os laváis** (fam.), - **Ustedes se lavan** (form.)
They wash themselves, they do wash themselves *or* they are washing themselves - **se lavan**

Future

SING. I shall wash myself - **me lavaré**
You will wash yourself - **te lavarás** (fam.), - **Usted se lavará** (form.)
He/she/it will wash him/her/itself - **se lavará**

PLUR. We shall wash ourselves - **nos lavaremos**
You will wash yourselves - **os lavaréis** (fam.), - **Ustedes se lavarán** (form.)
They will wash themselves - **se lavarán**

Past (Preterit)

SING. I washed myself *or* I did wash myself - **me lavé**
You washed yourself *or* you did wash yourself - **te lavaste** (fam.), - **Usted se lavó** (form.)
He/she/it washed him/her/itself *or* he/she/it did wash him/her/itself - **se lavó**

PLUR. We washed ourselves *or* we did wash ourselves - **nos lavamos**
You washed yourselves *or* you did wash yourselves - **os lavasteis** (fam.), - **Ustedes se lavaron** (form.)
They washed themselves *or* they did wash themselves - **se lavaron**

Past (Indefinite)

SING. I have washed myself - **me he lavado**
You haved washed yourself - **te has lavado** (fam.), - **Usted se ha lavado** (form.)
He/she/it has washed him/her/itself - **se ha lavado**

PLUR. We have washed ourselves - **nos hemos lavado**
You have washed yourselves - **os habéis lavado** (fam.), - **Ustedes se han lavado** (form.)
They have washed themselves - **se han lavado**

Past (Imperfect *or* Continuous)

SING. I was washing myself *or* I used to wash myself - **me lavaba**
You were washing yourself *or* you used to wash yourself - **te lavabas** (fam.), - **Usted se lavaba** (form.)
He/she/it was washing him/her/itself *or* he/she/it used to wash him/her/itself - **se lavaba**

PLUR. We were washing ourselves *or* we used to wash ourselves - **nos lavábamos**
You were washing yourselves *or* you used to wash yourselves - **os lavabais** (fam.), - **Ustedes se lavaban** (form.)
They were washing themselves *or* they used to wash themselves - **se lavaban**

Gerund

Washing oneself - **lavándose**

To Work - **Trabajar**
(Trab-ack-ar)

Present

SING. I work, I do work *or* I am working - **trabajo**
You work, you do work *or* you are working - **trabajas** (fam.), - **Usted trabaja** (form.)
He/she/it works, he/she/it does work *or* he/she/it is working - **trabaja**

PLUR. We work, we do work *or* we are working - **trabajamos**
You work, you do work *or* you are working - **trabajáis** (fam.), - **Ustedes trabajan** (form.)
They work, they do work *or* they are working - **trabajan**

Future

SING. I shall work - **trabajaré**
You will work - **trabajarás** (fam.), - **Usted trabajará** (form.)
He/she/it will work - **trabajará**

PLUR. We shall work - **trabajaremos**
You will work - **trabajaréis** (fam.), - **Ustedes trabajarán** (form.)
They will work - **trabajarán**

Past (Preterit)

SING. I worked *or* I did work - **trabajé**
You worked *or* you did work - **trabajaste** (fam.), - **Usted trabajó** (form.)
He/she/it worked *or* he/she/it did work - **trabajó**

PLUR. We worked *or* we did work - **trabajamos**
You worked *or* you did work - **trabajasteis** (fam.), - **Ustedes trabajaron** (form.)
They worked *or* they did work -**trabajaron**

Past (Indefinite)

SING. I have worked - **he trabajado**
You have worked - **has trabajado** (fam.), - **Usted ha trabajado** (form.)
He/she/it has worked - **ha trabajado**

PLUR. We have worked - **hemos trabajado**
You have worked - **habéis trabajado** (fam.), - **Ustedes han trabajado** (form.)
They have worked - **han trabajado**

Past (Imperfect *or* Continuous)

SING. I was working *or* I used to work - **trabajaba**
You were working *or* you used to work - **trabajabas** (fam.), - **Usted trabajaba** (form.)
He/she/it was working *or* he/she/it used to work - **trabajaba**

PLUR.We were working *or* we used to work - **trabajábamos**
You were working *or* you used to work - **trabajabais** (fam.), - **Ustedes trabajaban** (form.)
They were working *or* they used to work - **trabajaban**

Gerund

Working - **trabajando**

To Write - **Escribir**
(Es-kree-beer)

Present

SING. I write, I do write *or* I am writing - **escribo**
You write, you do write *or* you are writing - **escribes** (fam.), - **Usted escribe** (form.)
He/she/it writes, he/she/it does write *or* he/she/it is writing - **escribe**

PLUR. We write, we do write *or* we are writing - **escribimos**
You write, you do write *or* you are writing - **escribís** (fam.), - **Ustedes escriben** (form.)
They write, they do write *or* they are writing - **escriben**

Future

SING. I shall write - **escribiré**
You will write - **escribirás** (fam.), - **Usted escribirá** (form.)
He/she/it will write - **escribirá**

PLUR. We shall write - **escribiremos**
You will write - **escribiréis** (fam.), - **Ustedes escribirán**
They will write - **escribirán**

Past (Preterit)

SING. I wrote *or* I did write - **escribí**
You wrote *or* you did write - **escribiste** (fam.), - **Usted escribió** (form.)
He/she/it wrote *or* he/she/it did write - **escribió**

PLUR. We wrote *or* we did write - **escribimos**
You wrote *or* you did write - **escribisteis** (fam.), - **Ustedes escribieron** (form.)
They wrote *or* they did write - **escribieron**

Past (Indefinite)

SING. I have written - **he escrito**
You have written - **has escrito** (fam.), - **Usted ha escrito** (form.)
He/she/it has written - **ha escrito**

PLUR. We have written - **hemos escrito**
You have written - **habéis escrito** (fam.), - **Ustedes han escrito** (form.)
They have written - **han escrito**

Past (Imperfect *or* Continuous)

SING. I was writing *or* I used to write - **escribía**
You were writing *or* you used to write - **escribías** (fam.), - **Usted escribía** (form.)
He/she/it was writing *or* he/she/it used to write - **escribía**

PLUR. We were writing *or* we used to write - **escribíamos**
You were writing *or* you used to write - **escribíais** (fam.), - **Ustedes escribían** (form.)
They were writing *or* they used to write - **escribían**

Gerund

Writing - **escribiendo**

Four easily confused verbs

	Poder To be able	**Poner** To put	**Pedir** To ask for	**Perder** To lose
Present				
SING.	**Puedo**	**Pongo**	**Pido**	**Pierdo**
	Puedes	**Pones**	**Pides**	**Pierdes**
	Puede	**Pone**	**Pide**	**Pierde**
PLUR.	**Podemos**	**Ponemos**	**Pedimos**	**Perdemos**
	Podéis	**Ponéis**	**Pedís**	**Perdéis**
	Pueden	**Ponen**	**Piden**	**Pierden**
Future				
SING.	**Podré**	**Pondré**	**Pediré**	**Perderé**
	Podrás	**Pondrás**	**Pedirás**	**Perderás**
	Podrá	**Pondrá**	**Pedira**	**Perderá**
PLUR.	**Podremos**	**Pondremos**	**Pediremos**	**Perderemos**
	Podréis	**Pondréis**	**Pediréis**	**Perderéis**
	Podrán	**Pondrán**	**Pedirán**	**Perderán**
Past (Preterit)				
SING.	**Pude**	**Puse**	**Pedí**	**Perdí**
	Pudiste	**Pusiste**	**Pediste**	**Perdiste**
	Pudo	**Puso**	**Pidió**	**Perdió**
PLUR.	**Pudimos**	**Pusimos**	**Pedimos**	**Perdimos**
	Pudisteis	**Pusisteis**	**Pedisteis**	**Perdisteis**
	Pudieron	**Pusieron**	**Pidieron**	**Perdieron**
Past (Indefinite)				
SING	**He Podido**	**He Puesto**	**He Pedido**	**He Perdido**
	Has Podido	**Has Puesto**	**Has Pedido**	**Has Perdido**
	Ha Podido	**Ha Puesto**	**Ha Pedido**	**Ha Perdido**
PLUR.	**Hemos Podido**	**Hemos Puesto**	**Hemos Pedido**	**Hemos Perdido**
	Habéis Podido	**Habéis Puesto**	**Habéis Pedido**	**Habéis Perdido**
	Han Podido	**Han Puesto**	**Han Pedido**	**Han Perdido**
Past (Imperfect *or* Continuous)				
SING.	**Podía**	**Ponía**	**Pedía**	**Perdía**
	Podías	**Ponías**	**Pedías**	**Perdías**
	Podía	**Ponía**	**Pedía**	**Perdía**
PLUR.	**Podíamos**	**Poníamos**	**Pedíamos**	**Perdíamos**
	Podíais	**Poníais**	**Pedíais**	**Perdíais**
	Podían	**Ponían**	**Pedían**	**Perdían**
Gerunds				
	Pudiendo	**Poniendo**	**Pidiendo**	**Perdiendo**

Four more easily confused verbs

	Ir To go	Ver To see	Venir To come	Vestir To dress
Present				
SING.	**Voy**	**Veo**	**Vengo**	**Visto**
	Vas	**Ves**	**Vienes**	**Vistes**
	Va	**Ve**	**Viene**	**Viste**
PLUR.	**Vamos**	**Vemos**	**Venimos**	**Vestimos**
	Vais	**Veis**	**Venís**	**Vestís**
	Van	**Ven**	**Vienen**	**Visten**
Future				
SING.	**Iré**	**Veré**	**Vendré**	**Vestiré**
	Irás	**Verás**	**Vendrás**	**Vestirás**
	Irá	**Verá**	**Vendrá**	**Vestirá**
PLUR.	**Iremos**	**Veremos**	**Vendremos**	**Vestiremos**
	Iréis	**Veréis**	**Vendréis**	**Vestiréis**
	Irán	**Verán**	**Vendrán**	**Vestirán**
Past (Preterit)				
SING.	**Fui**	**Vi**	**Vine**	**Vestí**
	Fuiste	**Viste**	**Viniste**	**Vestiste**
	Fue	**Vio**	**Vino**	**Vistió**
PLUR.	**Fuimos**	**Vimos**	**Vinimos**	**Vestimos**
	Fuisteis	**Visteis**	**Vinisteis**	**Vestisteis**
	Fueron	**Vieron**	**Vinieron**	**Vistieron**
Past (Indefinite)				
SING.	**He Ido**	**He Visto**	**He Venido**	**He Vestido**
	Has Ido	**Has Visto**	**Has Venido**	**Has Vestido**
	Ha Ido	**Ha Visto**	**Ha Venido**	**Ha Vestido**
PLUR.	**Hemos Ido**	**Hemos Visto**	**Hemos Venido**	**Hemos Vestido**
	Habéis Ido	**Habéis Visto**	**Habéis Venido**	**Habéis Vestido**
	Han Ido	**Han Visto**	**Han Venido**	**Han Vestido**
Past (Imperfect *or* Continuous)				
SING.	**Iba**	**Veía**	**Venía**	**Vestía**
	Ibas	**Veías**	**Venías**	**Vestías**
	Iba	**Veía**	**Venía**	**Vestía**
PLUR.	**Íbamos**	**Veíamos**	**Veníamos**	**Vestíamos**
	Ibais	**Veíais**	**Veníais**	**Vestíais**
	Iban	**Veían**	**Venían**	**Vestían**
Gerunds				
	Yendo	**Viendo**	**Viniendo**	**Vistiendo**

Using two verbs together

When using two verbs in conjunction only the first one has to be varied according to the conjugations and the tense. For example; "Where can I obtain?" - **Dónde puedo obtener?** "Where can we obtain?" - **Dónde podemos obtener?"** "Where can they obtain?" - **Dónde pueden obtener?** The second verb remains in it's pure form i.e. **obtener.** More examples: "I am going to see" - **Voy a ver.** "We are going to see" - **Vamos a ver.** "He is going to see" - **Va a ver.** "I am going to make" - **Voy a hacer.** "We are going to play" - **Vamos a jugar.** "They are going to read" - **Van a leer.** "Can you help me?" - (fam.) - **Puedes ayudar me?** *or* **Me puedes ayudar?** (both are correct and mean exactly the same thing). "May I see?" - **Puedo ver?** "Would you like to see?" - (fam.) - **Quieres ver?** "We want to walk" - **Queremos andar.** "They want to eat" - **Quieren comer.** "They wanted to eat" - **Quisieron comer.** "They will want to eat" - **Querrán comer.**

The above does not apply however where the two verbs being used belong to different tenses, for instance "It is (present tense) paid" (past tense) - **Está pagado** *or* "It is done" - **Está hecho.** In this case we use the past participle as used in the Past (Indefinite) tense.

Forming a question

We have already formed some questions in the previous paragraph.
When you see a question written in Spanish you will note that it is normal to put an upside-down question mark at the start of the question as well as a normal one at the end.
As I have an English typewriter and my question mark is the right way up I am sure you will understand if I only put one at the end!
Turn to page 17 and we will form some questions using the verb To Be (**Ser).**
* Statement: "I am English" - **Soy Inglés.**
Statement: "You are Spanish" - (fam.) - **tú eres Español.** (form.) - **Usted es Español**
Question: "Are you Spanish?" - (fam.) - **eres tú Español?** (form.) - **es Usted Español?** To make it a question we do the same thing in Spanish as we do in English, we turn two words around - Statement: "You are", Question: "Are you?"
We also use the same inclination of voice as we do in English when asking a question.
Sometimes the statement and question do not need any changes except in tone of voice -
Statement: "They are big!" - **Son grandes!** Question: "Are they big?" - **Son grades?** Statement: "We are friends" - **Somos amigos.** Question "Are we friends?" - **Somos amigos?** Statement: "We were friends" - **Fuimos amigos.** Question: "Were you friends?" - **Fuisteis amigos?**
More useful questions:-
"How are you?" - (fam.) - **Como estás?** (form.) - **Como está Usted?**
"Do you understand?" - (fam.) - **Entiendes?** (form.) - **Entiende Usted?**
"Where can I change money?" - **Dónde puedo cambiar dinero?**
"Where is the bus station?" - **Dónde está la estación de autobús?**

"Is there a bus to ....?" - **Hay algún autobús para......?**
"What time does the next bus leave?" - **A qué hora sale el próximo autobús?**
"What is the price of a return ticket?" - **Quál es el precio de un billete de ida y vuelta?**
"Where can I hire a car?" - **Dónde puedo alquilar un coche?**
"Can you help me change the wheel?" - **Puede Usted ayudarme a cambiar la rueda?**
"How far is the next garage?" - **A qué distancia está el próximo garaje?**
"Can you repair it?" - **Puede Usted repararlo?** "When will it be ready?" - **Cuándo estará listo?** "How much do I owe you?" - **Cuánto le debo?**
"Could you write it down?" - **Puede escribirlo?** "Where are the toilets?" - **Dónde estan los servicios?** "May I see the menu?" - **Puedo ver la carta?**
"Would you bring us some bread?" - **Puede traernos pan?** "What do you recommend?" - **Qué recomienda?** "Have you any cigarettes?" - **Tiene cigarillos?** "and matches?" - **y fósforos?**
"Didn't I see you on the beach yesterday?" - **No te he visto en la playa ayer?**

* In Spanish capital letters are used for the names of countries but not nationalities. I have used them merely to make the phrases appear more familiar.

Reflexive verbs

A reflexive verb is a verb that describes an action that one can do to oneself, i.e. "I wash", there are many things that I can wash but when I wash myself the verb becomes reflexive. Many Spanish verbs are used in the reflexive form and to see how this works see pages 107 & 108, 24 & 25, 77 & 78 and 87.
You will see that we are now using a different set of pronouns, me - myself, **te** - (fam.) - yourself, **se** - (form.) - yourself, **nos** - ourselves, **os** - (fam.) - yourselves, and **se** (form) - yourselves *or* themselves.
It should be noted that the pronoun **se** used with a reflexive verb means oneself, yourself, himself, herself, itself, yourselves or themselves.
As with other pronouns, reflexive ones normally come before the verb but when the verb is used in it's pure form (infinitive) the pronoun comes after the verb and is attached to it, i.e. to wash oneself - **lavarse,** I wash myself - **me lavo,** I want to wash myself - **quiero lavarme.**
Having studied the pages of reflexive verbs it will make an interesting exercise to adapt one of the other verbs to it's reflexive form, for example **preguntar** (to ask) to **preguntarse** (to ask oneself)

Spanish is a language very rich in verbs and there are many alternatives available, as there are of course in English. You will find that different alternatives are used in different parts of the country.
The verbs that I have selected for you are those which should produce the minimum misunderstanding and at the same time be most easily remembered.

Dictionary of Verbs

A

	See Page
To abandon - **abandonar**	
To abate - **abatir**	
To abdicate - **abdicar**	
To abduct - **raptar**	
To abhor - **aborrecer**	
To be able - **poder**	19
To abolish - **abolir**	
To abort - **abortar**	
To abreviate - **abreviar**	
To absolve - **absolver**	
To absorb - **absorber**	
To abstain - **abstener**	
To abuse - **abusar**	
To accede - **acceder**	
To accelerate - **acelerar**	
To accentuate - **acentuar**	
To accept - **aceptar**	
To acclaim - **aclamar**	
To acclimatize - **aclimitar**	
To accommodate - **acomodar**	
To accompany - **acompañar**	
To accomplish - **realizar**	
To accost - **arimar**	
To account - **calcular**	
To accrue - **acrecentar**	
To accumulate - **acumular**	
To accuse - **acusar**	
To accustom - **acostumbrar**	
To be accustomed to - **soler**	
To ache - **doler**	10
To achieve - **conseguir**	44
To acknowledge - **reconocer**	
To acquaint - **informar**	
To be acquainted with - **conocer**	56
To acquire - **adquirir**	
To acquit - **absolver**	
To act (a part) - **desempeñar**	
To activate - **activar**	
To adapt - **adaptar**	
To add - **agregar**	
To addle - **pudrir**	
To address (a person) - **hablar a**	
To address (a letter) - **poner el destinario en un sobre**	
To adhere - **adherir**	
To adjoin - **juntar**	
To adjourn - **aplazar**	
To adjust - **arreglar**	13
To administer- **administrar**	
To admire - **admirar**	
To admit - **admitir**	
To adopt - **adoptar**	

	See Page
To adore - **adorar**	
To adorn - **adornar**	
To adulterate - **adulterar**	
To advance - **adelantar**	
To take advantage - **aprovechar**	
To advertise - **advertir**	
To advise - **aconsejar**	
To advocate - **abogar**	
To affect - **afectar**	
To affiliate - **afiliar**	
To affirm - **asegurar**	
To affix - **fijar**	
To afflict - **afligir**	
To age- **envejecer**	
To agravate - **agravar**	
To agitate - **agitar**	
To agonize - **atormentar**	
To agree - **acordar**	11
To aggrieve - **acongojar**	
To aid - **ayudar**	
To ail - **afligir**	
To aim - **apuntar**	
To air - **airear**	
To alarm - **alarmar**	
To alert - **alertar**	
To alienate - **enajenar**	
To align - **alinear**	
To allay - **calmar**	
To alege - **alegar**	
To alleviate - **aliviar**	
To allocate - **señalar**	
To allot - **asignar**	
To allow - **permitir**	
To allude - **aludir**	
To allure - **halagar**	
To ally - **aliar**	
To alter - **alterar**	
To alternate - **alternar**	
To amalgmate - **amalgamar**	
To amass - **acumular**	
To amaze - **asombrar**	
To amble - **amblar**	
To ambush - **emboscar**	
To amplify - **amplificar**	
To amputate - **amputar**	
To amuse - **divertir**	
To analyse - **analizar**	
To anchor - **anclar**	
To anger - **enfadar**	
To animate - **animar**	
To annex - **anexar**	
To annihilate - **destruir**	

A (cont.)

	See Page
To annotate - **anotar**	
To announce - **anunciar**	
To annoy - **molestar**	
To annul - **anular**	
To anoint - **untar**	
To answer - **contestar**	**12**
To anticipate - **anticipar**	
To apologise - **disculpar**	
To appaul - **espantar**	
To appeal - **apelar**	
To appear - **parecer**	**84**
To appease - **aplacar**	
To append - **añadir**	
To appertain - **pertenecer**	
To applaud - **aplaudir**	
To apply - **aplicar**	
To appoint - **apuntar**	
To appraise - **apreciar**	
To appreciate - **apreciar**	
To approach - **acercar**	
To approve - **aprobar**	
To approximate - **aproximar**	
To aprehend - **aprehender**	
To apropriate - **apropriar**	
To arbitrate - **arbitrar**	
To argue - **arguir**	
To arise - **subir**	
To arm - **armar**	
To arouse - **despertar**	
To arraign - **citar**	
To arrange - **arreglar**	**13**
To arrest - **detener**	
To arrive - **llegar**	**14**
To articulate - **articular**	
To ascend - **ascender**	
To ascribe - **atribuir**	
To ask - **preguntar**	**15**
To ask for - **pedir**	**16**
To aspire - **aspirar**	
To assault - **asaltar**	
To assemble - **congregar**	
To assert - **afirmar**	
To assent - **asentir**	
To assess - **estimar**	
To assign - **asignar**	
To assimilate - **asimilar**	
To assist - **ayudar**	
To associate - **asociar**	
To assume - **suponer**	**92**
To assure - **asegurar**	
To astonish - **asombrar**	
To atone - **expiar**	
To atribute - **atribuir**	
To attach - **conectar**	
To attack - **atacar**	
To attain - **conseguir**	**44**
To attempt - **intentar**	**101**
To attend - **atender**	
To attest - **certificar**	
To attract - **atrear**	
To attribute - **atribuir**	
To attume - **armonizar**	
To auction - **subastar**	
To audit - **intervenir**	
To augment - **aumentar**	
To authenticate - **autenticar**	
To authorize - **autorizar**	
To automate - **automatizar**	
To avenge - **vengar**	
To avert - **desviar**	
To avoid - **evitar**	
To avow - **declarar**	
To awake - **despertar**	
To award - **adjudicar**	

B

	See Page
To baffle - **frustrar**	
To bake - **cocer en horno**	
To balance - **equilibrar**	
To ban - **prohibir**	
To bang - **golpear**	**53**
To banish - **desterar**	
To baptise - **bautizar**	
To bar - **excluir**	
To bargain - **negociar**	
To barge - **irrumpir**	
To bark - **ladrar**	
To barter - **negociar**	
To baste - **pringar**	
To bathe - **bañar**	
To bathe oneself - **bañarse**	
To batter - **batir**	
To battle - **luchar**	
To be - **estar**	**18**
To be - **ser**	**17**
To beat *or* hit - **golpear**	**53**
To beat *(in a race)* - **ganar**	
To beat *(vanquish)* - **vencer**	
To bear *or* carry - **llevar**	**27**
To beckon - **hacer señas**	
To become - **ponerse**	**78**
To go to bed - **acostar**	
To bedeck - **adornar**	
To beg - **implorar**	

B (Cont.)

	See Page
To beget - **engendrar**	
To begin - **empezar**	**20**
To behave - **comportar**	
To behead - **decapitar**	
To behold - **mirar**	**64**
To bequeath - **legar**	
To bereave - **despojar**	
To belch - **eructar**	
To believe - **creer**	**21**
To belittle - **empequeñecer**	
To bellow - **mugir**	
To belong - **pertenecer**	
To bend - **inclinar**	
To benefit - **benificiar**	
To beseech - **rogar**	
To bestow - **conferir**	
To bet - **apostar**	
To betray - **traicionar**	
To better - **mejorar**	
To beware - **guardarse**	
To bewilder - **desconcertar**	
To bewitch - **hechizar**	
To bicker - **disputar**	
To bid - **ofrecer**	
To bide - **sufrir**	
To bill - **facturar**	
To billow - **ondular**	
To bind - **atar**	
To bite - **morder**	
To blackmail - **extorsionar**	
To blame - **culpar**	
To blare - **sonar con fuerza**	
To blaspheme - **blasfemar**	
To blaze - **inflamar**	
To bleach - **blanquear**	
To bleed - **sangrar**	
To blend - **mezclar**	
To bless - **bendecir**	
To blind - **cegar**	
To blink - **guiñar**	
To block - **bloquear**	
To bloom - **florecer**	
To blossom - **florecer**	
To blow - **soplar**	
To blunder - **tropezar**	
To blunt - **embotar**	
To blur - **manchar**	
To blush - **sonrojarse**	
To boast - **jactarse**	
To boil - **hervir**	
To bolt *(a door)* - **cerrar con cerrojo**	
To bomb - **bombardear**	
To book - **reservar**	
To border - **rayar**	
To bore *(be boring)* - **aburrir**	
To bore *(a hole)* - **barrenar**	
To be born - **nacer**	
To borrow - **pedir prestado**	
To bother - **molestar**	
To bottle - **embotellar**	
To bounce - **botar**	
To bow - **inclinar**	
To box in - **encajonar**	
To box *(sport)* - **boxear**	
To boycott - **boicotear**	
To brag - **jactarse**	
To brake *(while driving)* - **frenar**	
To break - **romper**	
To breakfast - **desayunar**	
To breathe - **respirar**	
To breed - **criar**	
To bring - **traer**	**22**
To brood over - **ruminar**	
To browse - **ramonear**	
To bruise - **magullar**	
To brush - **cepillar**	
To bubble - **burbujear**	
To bud - **brotar**	
To budge - **mover**	**68**
To buffet - **abofetear**	
To build - **construir**	
To bump - **golpear**	**53**
To bulge - **abultar**	
To bully - **abusar**	
To bunch together - **agrupear**	
To bundle - **liar**	
To buoy - **boyar**	
To burden - **cargar**	
To burn - **quemar**	
To burnish - **bruñir**	
To burrow - **excavar**	
To burst - **reventar**	
To bury - **enterrar**	
To bustle - **bullir**	
To butcher - **degollar**	
To butt - **topar**	
To button - **abotonar**	
To buy - **comprar**	**23**
To buzz - **zumbar**	

C

To cackle - **cacarear**	
To cage - **enjaular**	
To calculate - **calcular**	
To call - **llamar**	**24**
To call oneself - **llamarse**	**25**
To calm - **calmar**	

C (cont.)

	See Page
To camouflage - **camuflager**	
To camp - **acampar**	
'Can', *(To be able)* - **poder**	**19**
To cancel - **cancelar**	
To capitulate - **capitular**	
To capsize - **zozobrar**	
To captivate - **fascinar**	
To capture - **capturar**	
To care for - **cuidar**	**26**
To take care of - **cuidar**	**26**
To caress - **acariciar**	
To carpet - **alfombrar**	
To carry - **llevar**	**27**
To carve - **trinchar**	
To cast - **echar**	**74**
To catalogue - **catalogar**	
To catch - **coger**	
To cater - **proveer**	**76**
To cause - **causar**	
To caution - **prevenir**	
To cease - **cesar**	
To celebrate - **celebrar**	
To cement - **cementar**	
To censor - **censurar**	
To certify - **certificar**	
To challenge - **desafiar**	
To change - **cambiar**	
To charge *(a price)* - **encargar**	
To charm - **encantar**	
To chart - **poner en el mapa**	
To charter - **fletar**	
To chase - **perseguir**	
To chastise - **castigar**	
To chat - **charlar**	
To cheapen - **abaratar**	
To cheat - **engañar**	
To cheer *(up)* **alegrar**	
To cheer *(shout)* - **vitorear**	
To cherish - **amar**	
To chew - **mascar**	
To chill - **enfriar**	
To chime - **tañar**	
To chirp - **trinar**	
To chisel - **cincelar**	
To choke - **sofocar**	
To choose - **eligir**	
To chop - **cortar**	
To christen - **bautizar**	
To circulate - **circular**	
To civilize - **civilizar**	
To claim - **reclamar**	
To clap - **aplaudir**	
To clarify - **clarificar**	
To classify - **clasificar**	

	See Page
To clean - **limpiar**	
To climb - **escalar**	
To cling - **adherir**	
To close - **cerrar**	**28**
To clothe - **vestir**	**112**
To cloud - **obscurecer**	
To coach - **entrenar**	
To coagulate - **coagular**	
To coax - **halagar**	
To coexist - **coexistir**	
To cohabit - **cohabitar**	
To coil - **enrollar**	
To coin - **acuñar**	
To coincide - **coincidir**	
To be cold - **tener frio**	
To colonize - **colonizar**	
To collaborate - **colaborar**	
To collapse - **desplomer**	
To collect *(go and)* - **buscar**	**65**
To collide - **chocar**	
To comb - **peinar**	
To combat - **combatir**	
To combine - **combinar**	
To come - **venir**	**29**
To come back - **volver**	**81**
To come down - **bajar**	
To come in - **entrar**	**37**
To comfort - **confortar**	
To command - **ordenar**	
To commemorate - **conmemorar**	
To commence - **empezar**	**20**
To commend - **recomendar**	
To comment - **comentar**	
To commit - **cometer**	
To communicate - **comunicar**	
To commute - **commutar**	
To compare - **comparar**	
To compel - **obligar**	
To compensate - **compensar**	
To compete - **competir**	
To compile - **compilar**	
To complain - **quejarse**	
To complete - **completar**	
To complicate - **complicar**	
To compliment - **saludar**	
To comply - **ceder**	
To compose - **componer**	
To compound - **componer**	
To comprehend - **comprender**	
To compress - **comprimir**	
To comprise - **comprender**	
To compromise - **comprometer**	
To compute - **computar**	
To conceal - **ocultar**	

C (cont.)

	See Page
To concede - **conceder**	
To conceive - **concebir**	
To concentrate - **concentrar**	
To concern - **concernir**	
To concilliate - **conciliar**	
To conclude - **concluir**	
To concrete - **concretar**	
To concur - **concurrir**	
To condemn - **condenar**	
To condense - **condensar**	
To condescend - **condescender**	
To condition - **condicionar**	
To condone - **condonar**	
To conduct - **conducir**	**34**
To confer - **consultar**	
To confer *or* bestow - **conferir**	
To confess - **confesar**	
To confide - **confiar**	
To confine - **limitar**	
To confirm - **confirmar**	
To confiscate - **confiscar**	
To conform - **conformar**	
To confound - **confundir**	
To confront - **confrontar**	
To confuse - **confundir**	
To congeal - **coagular**	
To congest - **amontonar**	
To congratulate - **felicitar**	
To congregate - **congregar**	
To conjecture - **conjeturar**	
To conjugate - **conjugar**	
To conjure - **conjurar**	
To connect - **juntar**	
To connive - **consentir**	
To connote - **connotar**	
To conquer - **conquistar**	
To consecrate - **consagrar**	
To consent - **permitir**	
To conserve - **conservar**	
To consider - **considerar**	
To consign - **consignar**	
To consist - **consistir**	
To console - **consolar**	
To consolidate - **consolidar**	
To conspire - **conspirar**	
To constitute - **constituir**	
To construct - **construir**	
To consult - **consultar**	
To consumate - **consumar**	
To consume - **consumir**	
To contact - **poner en contacto con**	
To contain - **contener**	
To contaminate - **contaminar**	
To contemplate - **contemplar**	

	See Page
To contend - **disputar**	
To continue - **seguir**	**47**
To contract - **contratar**	
To contradict - **contradecir**	
To contrast - **contrastar**	
To contravene - **infringir**	
To contribute - **contribuir**	
To contrive - **inventar**	
To control - **controlar**	
To convalesce - **convalecer**	
To convene - **convocar**	
To converge - **converger**	
To converse - **conversar**	
To convert - **convertir**	
To convey - **transportar**	
To convict - **sentenciar**	
To convince - **persuadir**	
To cook - **cocinar**	
To cool - **refrescar**	
To co-ordinate - **coordinar**	
To co-operate - **cooperar**	
To copy - **copiar**	
To cordon off - **acordonar**	
To correct - **corregir**	
To correspond - **corresponder**	
To corroborate - **corroborar**	
To corrode - **corroer**	
To corrupt - **corromper**	
To cost - **costar**	
To cough - **toser**	
To court - **cortejar**	
To count - **contar**	**30**
To counterfeit - **falsificar**	
To countersign - **referendar**	
To cover - **cubrir**	
To crack - **rajar**	
To cram - **rellenar**	
To crash - **romper**	
To crawl - **arrastrar**	
To creak - **crujir**	
To crease - **arrugar**	
To create - **crear**	
To creep - **trepar**	
To credit - **acreditar**	
To cremate - **incinerar**	
To cripple - **lisiar**	
To criticize - **criticar**	
To croak - **graznar**	
To cross - **cruzar**	
To crouch - **agachar**	
To crowd - **amontar**	
To crown - **coronar**	
To crumble - **desmenuzar**	
To crunch - **crujir**	

C (cont.)

	See Page
To crush - **aplastar**	
To cry - **llorar**	
To cuddle - **abrazar**	
To culminate - **culminar**	
To cultivate - **cultivar**	
To curb - **poner freno**	
To curdle - **coagular**	
To cure - **curar**	
To curl - **ondular**	
To curse - **maldecir**	
To curtail - **cortar**	
To curtain - **cortinar**	
To curve - **encorvar**	
To cushion - **amortiguar**	
To cut - **cortar**	
To cycle - **ir en bicicleta**	

D

	See Page
To damage - **dañar**	
To damn - **maldecir**	
To dance - **bailar**	
To dangle - **colgar**	
To dare- **desafiar**	
To darken - **obscurecer**	
To darn - **zurcir**	
To dart *or* dash - **arrojar**	
To date *(make one)* - **citar**	
To date *(write one)* - **fechar**	
To daub - **untar**	
To daunt - **intimidar**	
To dawdle - **perder tiempo**	
To dawn - **amanecer**	
To daze *or* dazzle - **deslumbrar**	
To deaden - **amortiguar**	
To deafen - **ensordecer**	
To deal - **traficar en**	
To debase - **abatir**	
To debate - **debatir**	
To debit - **adeudar**	
To decay - **pudrir**	
To deceive - **engañar**	
To decide - **decidir**	**31**
To decimate - **diezmar**	
To decipher - **descifrar**	
To declare - **declarar**	
To decline - **declinar**	
To decompose - **pudrir**	
To decorate - **decorar**	
To decrease - **disminuir**	
To decree - **decretar**	
To decry - **desacreditar**	
To dedicate - **dedicar**	
To deduce - **deducir**	
To deduct - **deducir**	
To deface - **desfigurar**	
To defame - **difamar**	
To default - **faltar**	
To defeat - **vencer**	
To defend - **defender**	
To defile - **manchar**	
To define - **definir**	
To deflate - **desinflar**	
To deflect - **desviar**	
To deform - **deformar**	
To defraud - **defraudar**	
To defy - **desafiar**	
To degenerate - **degenerar**	
To degrade - **degradar**	
To delay - **diferir**	
To delegate - **delegar**	
To delete - **tachar**	
To delight - **deleitar**	
To deliver - **entregar**	
To demand - **demandar**	
To demolish - **demoler**	
To demonstrate - **demonstrar**	
To demoralize - **desmoralizar**	
To denote - **denotar**	
To denounce - **denunciar**	
To dent - **abollar**	
To deny - **negar**	
To depart - **marchar**	**58**
To depend - **depender**	
To deplore - **deplorar**	
To deploy - **desplegar**	
To deport - **deportar**	
To deposit - **depositar**	
To deprave - **depravar**	
To depreciate - **rebajar**	
To depress - **deprimar**	
To deprive - **privar**	
To deride - **burlar**	
To derive - **derivar**	
To descend - **descender**	
To describe - **describir**	
To desert - **desertar**	
To deserve - **merecer**	
To design - **proyectar**	
To designate - **designar**	
To desire - **desear**	
To desist - **desistir**	
To despair - **desperar**	
To despatch - **despatchar**	
To despise - **despreciar**	
To destine - **destinar**	
To detach - **desprender**	

D (cont.)

	See Page
To destroy - **destruir**	
To detain - **detener**	
To detect - **descubrir**	
To deter - **disuadir**	
To deteriorate - **deteriorar**	
To determine - **determinar**	
To detest - **detestar**	
To detonate - **detonar**	
To detract - **detraer**	
To devalue - **desvalorizar**	
To devastate - **devastar**	
To develop - **desarrollar**	
To deviate - **desviar**	
To devise - **inventar**	
To devote - **dedicar**	
To devour - **devorar**	
To diagnose - **diagnosticar**	
To dial *(phone)* - **marcar el numero**	
To dictate - **dictar**	
To die - **morir**	
To differ - **diferenciar**	
To diffuse - **difundir**	
To dig - **cavar**	
To digest - **digerir**	
To digress - **divigar**	
To dilate - **dilatar**	
To dilute - **diluir**	
To diminish - **disminuir**	
To dine - **cenar**	
To dip- **sumergir**	
To direct - **dirigir**	
To disable - **incapacitar**	
To disagree - **disentir**	
To disappear - **desaparecer**	
To disappoint - **frustrar**	
To disapprove - **desaprobar**	
To disarm - **desarmar**	
To disarrange - **desordenar**	
To disband - **dispersar**	
To disbelieve - **descreer**	
To discard - **desechar**	
To discern - **discernir**	
To discharge - **descargar**	
To discipline - **disciplinar**	
To disclaim - **repudiar**	
To disclose - **descubrir**	
To disconnect - **desconectar**	
To discontinue - **descontinuar**	
To discount - **descontar**	
To discourage - **desalantar**	
To discover - **descubrir**	
To discredit - **desacreditar**	
To discriminate - **discriminar**	

	See Page
To discuss - **discutir**	
To disembark - **desembarcar**	
To disfigure - **desfigurar**	
To disgrace - **deshonrar**	
To disguise - **disfrazar**	
To disgust - **repugnar**	
To dishearten - **desilusionar**	
To dishonour - **deshonrar**	
To disinfect - **desinfectar**	
To disintegrate - **desintegrar**	
To dislike - **no gustar**	**60**
To dislocate - **dislocar**	
To dislodge - **desalojar**	
To dismantle - **desmantelar**	
To dismay - **desanimar**	
To dismember - **desmembrar**	
To dismiss - **despedir**	
To dismount - **desmontar**	
To disobey - **desobedecer**	
To disown - **renunciar**	
To dispel - **disipiar**	
To dispense - **dispensar**	
To disperse - **dispersar**	
To displace - **desplazar**	
To display - **exhibir**	
To displease - **desagredar**	
To dispose - **disponer**	
To disprove - **refutar**	
To dispute - **disputar**	
To disqualify - **descalificar**	
To disregard - **ignorar**	
To disrespect - **desacatar**	
To disrupt - **trastornar**	
To dissatisfy - **desatisfacer**	
To dissent - **disentir**	
To dissolve - **disolver**	
To dissuade - **disuadir**	
To distil - **destilar**	
To distort - **falsear**	
To distract - **distraer**	
To distress - **afligir**	
To distribute - **distribuir**	
To distrust - **desconfiar de**	
To disturb - **molestar**	
To dive - **sumergir**	
To divert - **divertir**	
To divide - **dividir**	
To divorce - **divorciar**	
To divulge - **divulgar**	
To do - **hacer**	**32**
To dodge - **eludir**	
To domesticate - **domesticar**	
To dominate - **dominar**	

D (cont.)

	See Page
To donate - **donar**	
To have done - **haber**	
To double - **doblar**	
To doubt - **dudar**	
To drag - **arrastrar**	
To draw *(pictures)* - **dibujar**	
To dream - **soñar**	
To dress - **vestir**	**112**
To drill *(holes)* - **taladrar**	
To drink - **beber**	**33**
To drip - **gotear**	
To drive *(a car)* - **conducir**	**34**
To droop - **bajar**	
To drop - **dejar caer**	
To drown - **ahogar**	
To dry - **secar**	
To duplicte - **duplicar**	
To dwell - **habitar**	
To dwindle - **disminuir**	
To dye - **teñir**	

E

	See Page
To earn - **ganar**	
To ease - **aliviar**	
To eat - **comer**	**35**
To eavesdrop - **fisgonear**	
To echo - **resonar**	
To eclipse - **eclipsar**	
To edit - **editar**	
To educate - **educar**	
To efface - **borrar**	
To effect - **efectuar**	
To effuse - **derramar**	
To eject - **echar**	**74**
To elaborate - **elaborar**	
To elapse - **pasar**	
To elate - **exaltar**	
To elect - **elegir**	
To electrify - **electrizar**	
To electrocute - **electrocutar**	
To elevate - **elevar**	
To elicit - **educir**	
To eliminate - **eliminar**	
To elope - **escapar**	
To elude - **eludir**	
To emanate - **emanar**	
To emancipate - **emancipar**	
To embark - **embarcar**	
To embarrass - **desconcertar**	
To embezzle - **desfalcar**	
To embody - **incorporar**	
To emboss - **relevar**	
To embrace - **abrazar**	
To embroider - **bordar**	
To emerge - **surgir**	
To emigrate - **emigrar**	
To emit - **emitir**	
To emphasize - **acentuar**	
To employ - **emplear**	
To empty - **vaciar**	
To emulate - **emular**	
To enable - **habilitar**	
To enact - **establecer**	
To enamel - **esmaltar**	
To encamp - **acampar**	
To encase - **encajonar**	
To enchant - **encantar**	
To encircle - **cercar**	
To enclose - **circundar**	
To encompass - **abarcar**	
To encounter - **encontrar**	**40**
To encourage - **animar**	
To encroach - **usurpar**	
To end - **terminar**	**41**
To endanger - **poner en peligro**	
To endear - **hacer querer**	
To endeavor - **intentar**	**101**
To endorse - **autorizar**	
To endow - **dotar**	
To endure - **sufrir**	
To enforce - **forzar**	
To engage - **ocupar**	
To engender - **engendrar**	
To engineer - **dirigir**	
To engrave - **grabar**	
To engross - **absorber**	
To enhance - **mejorar**	
To enjoy - **gozar**	**36**
To enlarge - **aumentar**	
To enlighten - **enseñar**	**96**
To enlist - **alistar**	
To enliven - **alegrar**	
To enmesh - **enredar**	
To enquire - **preguntar**	**15**
To enrage - **enfurecer**	
To enrich - **enriquecer**	
To enrol - **alistar**	
To enslave - **esclavizar**	
To ensure - **asegurar**	
To entail - **vincular**	
To entangle - **enredar**	
To enter - **entrar**	**37**
To entertain - **divertir**	
To enthral - **encantar**	
To enthuse - **entusiasmar**	
To entice - **tentar**	

E (cont.)

	See Page
To entrench - **atrincherar**	
To entwine - **entrelazar**	
To enumerate - **enumerar**	
To enunciate - **enunciar**	
To envelop - **envolver**	
To envisage - **imaginar**	
To envy - **envidiar**	
To equal - **igualar**	
To equate - **igualar**	
To equip - **equipar**	
To eradicate - **erradicar**	
To erase - **borrar**	
To erect - **erigir**	
To erode - **erosionar**	
To err - **errar**	
To erupt - **prorrumpir**	
To escalate - **escalar**	
To escape - **escapar**	
To escort - **acompañar**	
To establish - **establecer**	
To estimate - **estimar**	
To evacuate - **evacuar**	
To evade - **evadir**	
To evaluate - **evaluar**	
To evaporate - **evaporar**	
To even - **nivelar**	
To evict - **desahuciar**	
To evoke - **evocar**	
To evolve - **desarrolar**	
To exalt - **exaltar**	
To examine - **examinar**	
To exasperate - **exasperar**	
To excavate - **excavar**	
To exceed - **exceder**	
To excel - **aventajar**	
To exchange - **cambiar**	
To excite - **excitar**	
To exclaim - **exclamar**	
To exclude - **excluir**	
To excuse - **excusar**	
To execute - **ejecutar**	
To exempt - **exentar**	
To exercise - **ejercitar**	
To exert - **esforzar**	
To exhale - **exhalar**	
To exhaust - **agotar**	
To exhibit - **exhibir**	
To exhilarate - **alegrar**	
To exhume - **exhumar**	
To exile - **desterrar**	
To exist - **existir**	
To exit - **salir**	**48**
To expand - **estender**	
To expect - **esperar**	**104**
To expedite - **expedir**	
To expel - **expulsar**	
To expend - **gastar**	
To experience - **experimentar**	
To experiment - **experimentar**	
To expire - **expirar**	
To explain - **explicar**	
To explode - **explotar**	
To exploit - **explotar**	
To explore - **explorar**	
To export - **exportar**	
To expose - **exponer**	
To expound - **exponer**	
To express - **expresar**	
To extend - **extender**	
To extenuate - **mitigar**	
To exterminate - **exterminar**	
To extinguish - **extinguir**	
To extol - **enaltecer**	
To extol - **enaltecer**	
To extort - **extorsionar**	
To extract - **extractar**	

F

	See Page
To fabricate - **fabricar**	
To face - **afrontar**	
To facilitate - **facilitar**	
To fade - **palidecer**	
To fail - **faltar**	
To faint - **desfallecer**	
To fall - **caer**	**38**
To falsify - **falsificar**	
To falter - **vacilar**	
To fan - **abanicar**	
To fancy - **encaprichar**	
To fantasize - **imaginar**	
To farm - **cultivar**	
To fascinate - **fascinar**	
To fashion - **amoldar**	
To fast - **ayunar**	
To fasten - **abrochar**	
To father - **adoptar**	
To fathom - **sondar**	
To fatigue - **fatigar**	
To fatten - **engordar**	
To fault - **faltar**	
To favour - **favorecer**	
To fawn - **adular**	
To fear - **temer**	
To feast - **festejar**	
To feature - **representar**	
To feed - **alimentar**	
To feel - **sentir**	**39**

F (cont.)

	See Page
To feign - **fingir**	
To fence - **cercar**	
To ferment - **fermentar**	
To ferry - **cruzar**	
To fertilize - **fertilizar**	
To fester- **supurar**	
To fetch - **traer**	**22**
To fetter - **encadenar**	
To feud - **enfeudar**	
To fidget - **molestar**	
To fight - **luchar**	
To filch - **sisar**	
To file *(workshop)* - **limar**	
To file *(office)* - **archivar**	
To file in - **entrar en fila**	
To file out - **salir en fila**	
To fill - **llenar**	
To fillet - **filetear**	
To film - **filmar**	
To filter - **filtrar**	
To finance - **financiar**	
To find - **encontrar**	**40**
To fine *(make pay)* - **multar**	
To finger - **tocar**	**98**
To finish - **terminar**	**41**
To fire *(a gun)* - **disparar**	
To fire - **encender**	
To fish - **pescar**	
To fit - **acoplar**	
To fit - **instalar**	
To fit in - **encajar**	
To fix - **fijar**	
To flag - **debilitar**	
To flake off - **desconchar**	
To flame *or* flare up - **inflamar**	
To flatten - **aplanar**	
To flatter - **adular**	
To flaunt - **ostentar**	
To flavour - **sazonar**	
To flaw - **estropear**	
To flee - **huir**	
To flex - **flexionar**	
To flicker - **fluctuar**	
To flinch - **recular**	
To fling - **lanzar**	
To flirt - **coquetear**	
To float - **flotar**	
To flock - **congregar**	
To flog - **azotar**	
To flood - **inundar**	
To flop - **caer**	**38**
To flounder - **vacilar**	
To flourish - **florecer**	

	See Page
To flout - **despreciar**	
To flow - **fluir**	
To flower - **florecer**	
To fluctuate - **fluctuar**	
To flush *or* blush - **sonrojar**	
To flush *(as with water)* - **derramar**	
To flutter - **aletear**	
To fly - **volar**	**42**
To foam - **espumar**	
To focus - **enfocar**	
To fog - **obscurecer**	
To foil - **frustrar**	
To fold - **doblar**	
To follow - **seguir**	**47**
To foment - **fomentar**	
To fondle - **acariciar**	
To fool *or* trick - **engañar**	
To fool about - **hacer el tonto**	
To forage - **forrajear**	
To forbear - **abstenerse**	
To forbid - **prohibir**	
To force - **forzar**	
To ford - **vadear**	
To forecast - **pronosticar**	
To forego - **abstenerse de**	
To foresee - **prever**	
To forestall - **prevenir**	
To foretell - **predecir**	
To forfeit - **perder**	**66**
To forge *(in metal etc.)* - **forjar**	
To forge *(documents etc.)* - **falsificar**	
To forget - **olvidar**	**43**
To forgive - **perdonar**	
To form - **formar**	
To formulate - **formular**	
To fornicate - **fornicar**	
To forsake - **dejar**	**59**
To fortify - **fortificar**	
To fossilize - **fosilizar**	
To foster - **cuidar**	**26**
To foul *(break the rules)* - **violar las reglas**	
To foul *(make dirty)* - **ensuciar**	
To found - **fundar**	
To fracture - **fracturar**	
To frame *(as a picture)* - **encuadrar**	
To free - **libertar**	
To freeze - **helar**	
To frequent - **frecuentar**	
To fret - **preocuparse**	
To frighten - **asustar**	
To frisk *or* frolic - **retozar**	
To fritter - **disipar**	

F (cont.)

	See Page
To frizzle - **rizar**	
To froth - **espumar**	
To frown - **fruncir**	
To frustrate - **frustar**	
To fry - **freir**	
To fulfil - **realizar**	
To fume - **ahumar**	
To fumigate - **fumigar**	
To function - **funcionar**	
To fund - **invertir**	
To furnish *(provide)* - **proveer**	**76**
To furnish *(furniture)* - **amueblar**	
To fuse together - **fundir**	
To fuss - **alborotar**	

G

	See Page
To gag - **amordazar**	
To gain - **ganar**	
To gallop - **galopar**	
To gamble - **jugar**	**73**
To gamble *(with money)* - **jugar dinero**	
To gamble *or* risk - **arriesgar**	
To gambol - **brincar**	
To gape - **bostezar**	
To gargle - **gargarizar**	
To garnish - **adornar**	
To gas - **asfixiar con gas**	
To gasp - **boquear**	
To gather *(people, together)* - **reunir**	
To gather *(flowers etc.)* - **recoger**	
To gauge - **calibrar**	
To gaze - **mirar**	**64**
To generalize - **generalizar**	
To generate - **engendrar**	
To germinate - **germinar**	
To gesticulate - **gesticular**	
To gesture - **gesticular**	
To get - **conseguir**	**44**
To get away - **escapar**	
Get away! - **largo!**	
To get back *or* return to - **volver**	**81**
To get back *or* recover - **recobrar**	
To get down - **bajar**	
To get off - **desmontar**	
To get on *or* proceed - **seguir**	**47**
Get out! - **fuera!**	
To get out *(ones purse etc.)* - **sacar**	**94**
To get ready - **preparar**	
To get sick - **ponerse**	**78**
To get up - **levantar**	
To giggle - **reir**	
To give - **dar**	**45**
To gladden - **alegrar**	
To glance - **mirar**	**64**
To glare *or* shine - **brillar**	
To glare *(facially)* - **mirar con indignación**	
To glass *or* glaze - **acristalar**	
To gleam - **brillar**	
To glean - **espigar**	
To glide - **planear**	
To glimpse - **ver rápidamente**	
To gline - **reflejar**	
To glisten *or* glitter - **brillar**	
To gloat - **gozarse**	
To glorify - **glorificar**	
To gloss - **lustrar**	
To glow - **relucir**	
To glue - **encolar**	
To gnash - **crujir**	
To gnaw - **roer**	
To go - **ir**	**46**
To go and get - **buscar**	**65**
To go away - **marchar**	**58**
Go away! - **vaya!**	
To go back - **volver**	**81**
To go down - **bajar**	
To go in - **entrar**	**37**
To go on - **seguir**	**47**
To go out - **salir**	**48**
To go past - **pasar**	
To go shopping - **ir de compras**	
To go up - **subir**	
To goad - **incitar**	
To gobble *or* gorge - **engullir**	
To gossip - **chismear**	
To govern - **gobernar**	
To grab - **coger**	
To grade - **graduar**	
To graduate - **graduar**	
To graft on - **empalmar**	
To grant - **dar**	**45**
To granulate - **granular**	
To grapple - **luchar**	
To grasp - **coger**	
To grate - **rallar**	
To gratify - **gratificar**	
To gravitate - **gravitar**	
To graze *(as cattle)* - **pastorear**	
To graze *(the skin)* - **raspar**	
To grease - **engrasar**	
To greet - **saludar**	
To grieve - **lamentar**	
To grill - **asar en parrilla**	
To grimace - **hacer mueca**	
To grin - **sonreir**	

G (cont.)

See Page

To grind - **moler**
To grip - **agarrar**
To gripe - **quejarse**
To groan - **gruñir**
To groom - **preperar**
To grope - **palpar**
To group - **agrupar**
To grow - **crecer**
To growl - **gruñir**
To grudge - **envidiar**
To grumble - **quejarse**
To grunt - **gruñir**
To guarantee - **garantizar**
To guard - **guardar**
To guess - **adivinar**
To guide - **guiar**
To gulp - **engullir**
To gurgle - **gorgotear**
To gush - **derramar**
To gut - **destripar**

H

To hack - **cortar**
To haggle - **regatear**
To hail - **saludar**
To hail *(storm)* - **granizar**
To halt - **parar** **91**
To halve - **dividir en dos**
To hammer - **martillar**
To hamper - **estorbar**
To hand - **pasar por mano**
To handcuff - **maniatar**
To handicap - **impedir**
To handle - **manejar**
To hang - **suspender**
To hanker - **ansiar**
To happen - **suceder** **49**
To harangue - **arengar**
To harass - **hostigar**
To harbour - **hospedar**
To harden - **endurecer**
To harm - **dañar**
To harmonize - **armonizar**
To harness - **enganchar**
To harvest - **cosechar**
To hatch - **incubar**
To hate - **detestar**
To haul - **arrastrar**
To haunt - **frecuentar**
To have - **tener** **50**
To have *(something to eat or drink)* - **tomar** **93**
To have done *(something)* - **haber**

See Page

To have done with - **desentenderse de**
To have to - **tener que** **51**
To have to be - **tener que ser**
I have been etc. - **he ido etc.** **46**
To have to go - **tener que ir**
To hazard - **arriesgar**
To head *or* lead - **encabezar**
To heal - **curar**
To heap - **amontonar**
To hear - **oír** **52**
To heat - **calentar**
To heave *(rise and fall)* - **levantar y bajar**
To heave *(pull)*- **arrastrar**
To heave to *(Nautical)* - **poner al pairo**
To heed - **escuchar** **52**
To heel *(shoes)* - **poner tacones**
To heighten - **levantar**
To help - **ayudar**
Help! - **socorro!**
To help oneself - **servirse**
To hem - **dobladillar**
To hemorrhage - **sangrar**
To herald - **anunciar**
To herd - **agrupar**
To hesitate - **vacilar**
To hew - **cortar**
To hibernate - **invernar**
To hide - **ocultar**
To hike - **andar** **105**
To hitch hike - **viajar en auto-stop**
To hinder - **impedir**
To hinge - **engoznar**
To hint - **insinuar**
To hire - **alquilar**
To hiss - **sisear**
To hit - **golpear** **53**
To hitch - **acoplar**
To hoard - **atesorar**
To hoax - **chasquear**
To hobble *(as a horse)* - **manear**
To hobble *or* limp - **cojear**
To hoe - **azadonar**
To hoist - **elevar**
To hold *or* have - **tener** **50**
To hold *or* contain - **contener**
To hole - **perforar**
To holiday - **hacer vacaciones**
To hollow - **excavar**
To hone - **afilar**
To honour - **honrar**
To hoodwink - **engañar**
To hook - **enganchar**

H (cont.)

See Page

To hoot *(car horn)* - **tocar la bocina**
To hop - **brincar**
To hope - **esperar** **104**
To horrify - **horrorizar**
To hose - **regar con manguera**
To house - **albergar**
To hover - **volar** **42**
To howl - **chillar**
To huddle - **amontonar**
To hug - **abrazar**
To hum - **zumbar**
To humble *or* humiliate - **humilliar**
To humour - **mimar**
To hunger - **tener hambre**
To hunt - **cazar**
To hurdle - **saltar vallas**
To hurl - **lanzar**
To hurry - **tener prisa**
To hurt - **doler** **10**
To hurt *or* harm - **dañar**
To hustle - **apresurar**
To hypnotize - **hipnotizar**

I

To ice - **helar**
To identify - **identificar**
To idle - **holgazanear**
To ignite - **encender**
To ignore - **ignorar**
To become ill - **enfermar**
To illuminate - **iluminar**
To illustrate - **ilustrar**
To imagine - **imaginar**
To imbibe - **beber** **33**
To imitate - **imitar**
To immigrate - **inmigrar**
To immortalize - **inmortalizar**
To immunize - **inmunizar**
To impair - **debilitar**
To impart - **impartir**
To impeach - **acusar**
To impede - **impedir**
To impel - **impeler**
To impend - **pender**
To imperil - **poner en peligro**
To impersonate - **impersonar**
To implant - **implantar**
To implement - **llevar a cabo**
To implicate - **implicar**
To implore - **implorar**
To imply - **implicar**
To import - **importar**
To importune - **importunar**

See Page

To impose - **imponer**
To impoverish - **empobrecer**
To impregnate - **impregnar**
To impress - **impresionar**
To imprint - **imprimir**
To imprison - **encarcelar**
To improve - **mejorar**
To improvise - **improvisar**
To impugn - **impugnar**
To impute - **imputar**
To inuagerate - **inaugurar**
To incapacitate - **incapacitar**
To incense - **incensar**
To incinerate - **incinerar**
To incise - **cortar**
To incite - **incitar**
To incline - **inclinar**
To include - **incluir**
To incorporate - **incorporar**
To increase - **aumentar**
To incubate - **incubar**
To incur - **incurrir**
To indemnify - **indemnizar**
To indent - **dentar**
To index - **poner indice**
To indicate - **indicar**
To indict - **acusar**
To indispose - **indisponer**
To individualize - **individualizar**
To indoctrinate - **enseñar** **96**
To indorse - **endorsar**
To induce *or* induct - **inducir**
To indulge - **consentir**
To indulge oneself - **entregarse**
To industrialize - **industrializar**
To inebriate - **emborrachar**
To infect - **infectar**
To infer - **inferir**
To infest - **infestar**
To infiltrate - **infiltrar**
To inflame - **inflamar**
To inflate - **inflar**
To inflict - **infligir**
To influence - **influir**
To inform - **informar**
To infringe - **infringir**
To infuriate - **enfurecer**
To infuse - **infundir**
To ingratiate - **congraciarse**
To inhabit - **habitar**
To inhale - **inhalar**
To inherit - **heredar**
To inhibit - **inhibir**
To initial - **poner iniciales**

See Page

To initiate - **iniciar**
To inject - **inyectar**
To injure - **herir**
To inlay - **embutir**
To innovate - **innovar**
To inoculate - **inocular**
To inquire - **preguntar** 15
To inscribe - **inscribir**
To insert - **insertar**
To insinuate - **insinuar**
To insist - **insistir**
To inspect - **examinar**
To inspire - **inspirar**
To install - **instalar**
To instigate - **instigar**
To instill - **instilar**
To institute - **instituir**
To instruct - **instruir**
To insulate - **aislar**
To insult - **insultar**
To insure - **asegurar**
To ingegrate - **integrar**
To intend - **intentar** 101
To intensify - **intensificar**
To inter - **enterrar**
To intercede - **interceder**
To intercept - **interceptar**
To interchange - **intercambiar**
To interest - **interesar**
To interfere - **interferir**
To interlace *or* interlock - **entrelezar**
To intermingle *or* intermix - **entremezclar**
To interpret - **interpretar**
To interrogate - **interrogar**
To interupt - **interrumpir**
To intersect - **entrecortar**
To intertwine - **entrelezar**
To intervene - **intervenir**
To interview - **entrevistar**
To intimate - **intimar**
To intimidate -**intimidar**
To intone - **entonar**
To intoxicate - **intoxicar**
To intrench - **atrincherar**
To intrigue - **intrigar**
To introduce *(put in)* - **introducir**
To introduce *(people)* - **presentar**
To intrude - **entremeter**
To inundate - **inundar**
To invade - **invadir**
To invalidate - **invalidar**
To invent - **inventar**

See Page

To invest - **invertir**
To investigate - **investigar**
To invigorate - **vigorizar**
To invite - **invitar**
To invoice - **facturar**
To invoke - **invocar**
To involve - **envolver**
To irk - **fastidiar**
To iron - **planchar**
To irradiate - **irradiar**
To irrigate - **irrigar**
To irritate - **irritar**
To isolate - **separar**
To issue - **publicar**
To itch - **picar**
To itemize - **detallar**

J

To jab - **pinchar**
To jack up - **levantar con gato**
To jail - **encarcelar**
To jam - **atascar**
To jar *or* jolt - **sacudir**
To jeer - **burlar**
To jeopardize - **arriesgar**
To jerk - **sacudir**
To jest - **bromear**
To jettison - **echar** 74
To jog *or* jolt - **sacudir**
To go jogging - **estimularse**
To join - **unir**
To joke - **bromear**
To jolt - **sacudir**
To jot - **anotar**
To journey - **viajar** 100
To judge *(sit in judgement)* - **juzgar**
To judge - **estimar**
To juggle - **escamotear**
To jumble - **mezclar**
To jump - **saltar**
To justify - **justificar**
To jut out - **proyectar**

K

To keep - **retener** 54
To keep on - **seguir** 47
To keep out - **impedir la entrada**
To keep up - **mantener**
To kennel - **poner en perrera**
To kick - **cocear**
To kidnap - **secuestrar**
To kill - **matar**

K (cont.)

See Page

To kindle - **encender**
To kiss - **besar**
To knead - **masar**
To kneel - **arrodillarse**
To knife - **acuchillar**
To knight - **condecorar**
To knit - **calcetar**
To knock - **golpear** **53**
To knot - **anundar**
To know *(how)* - **saber** **55**
To know *(be acquainted with)* -**conocer** **56**

L

To label - **etiquetar**
To labour - **trabajar** **109**
To lace - **abrochar**
To lack - **faltar**
To lacquer - **dar laca**
To ladle - **servir con cucharón**
To lag *(as a boiler)* - **proteger**
To lag *(behind)* - **retrasar**
To lament - **lamentar**
To laminate - **laminar**
To lance - **lancear**
To land - **aterrizar**
To languish - **languidecer**
To lap over *(overlap)* - **extender**
To lap over *(overflow)* - **inundar**
To lap *(as a cat)* - **beber con la lengua**
To lap up *(relish)* - **relamarse de gusto**
To lapse *or* elapse - **transcurrir**
To lapse *or* weaken - **decaer**
To lash *or* strike - **azotar**
To lash together - **atar**
To lasso - **lazar**
To last - **durar**
To latch *(as a door)* - **cerrar con pasador**
To latch on to - **unir**
To lather - **enjabonar**
To laud - **alabar**
To laugh - **reir**
To launch *(a boat or ship)* - **botar**
To launch *(a projectile)* - **lanzar**
To launch *(a business or idea)* - **principiar**
To launder - **lavar y planchar** **107**
To lavish - **prodigar**
To lay - **poner** **77**
To lay aside - **poner a un lado**
To lay down *(legislate)* - **legislar**

See Page

To lay down *or* put to bed - **acostar**
To laze - **holgazanear**
To lead - **conducir** **34**
To leak - **gotear**
To lean - **apoyar**
To leap - **saltar**
To learn - **aprender** **57**
To lease - **arrendar**
To leave *or* depart - **marchar** **58**
To leave *or* depart *(trains etc.)* - **salir** **48**
To leave alone - **dejar** **59**
To leave behind - **dejar atrás**
Leave it! - **deja lo!**
To leave out - **omitir**
To leave outside - **dejar fuera**
To lecture - **enseñar** **96**
To legalize - **legalizar**
To legislate - **legislar**
To lend - **prestar**
To lengthen - **alargar**
To lessen - **disminuar**
To let *or* allow - **permitir**
To let alone *or* let be - **dejar** **59**
To let *(for rent)* - **alquilar**
To level - **nivelar**
To lever - **apalancar**
To levy - **recaudar**
To liberate - **liberar**
To licence - **licenciar**
To lick - **lamer**
To lie *or* deceive - **mentir**
To lie down - **acostar**
To lift - **levantar**
To light - **encender**
To lighten *(the darkness)* - **iluminar**
To lighten *(the load)* - **aliviar**
To lighten *(the weight)* - **aligerar**
To like - **gustar** **60**
To like to have - **querer** **106**
To liken - **comparar**
To limber up - **pre-calentarse**
To limit - **limitar**
To limp - **cojear**
To line up - **poner en fila**
To line *(clothing etc.)* - **forrar**
To linger - **tardar**
To link - **enlazar**
To liquidate - **liquidar**
To lisp - **cecear**
To list *(make one)* - **registrar**
To list *(prices)* - **cotizar**
To list *(as a ship)* - **escorar**

L (cont.)

See Page

To listen - **escuchar** 62
To litigate - **litigar**
To litter - **esparcir**
To live - **vivir** 63
To load - **cargar**
To loaf - **holgazanear**
To loan - **prestar**
To loathe - **aborrecer**
To lobby - **cabildear**
To locate - **encontrar** 40
To lock - **cerrar con llave** 28
To lodge - **alojar**
To lodge *(be housed)* - **hospedar**
To log *(as in a book)* - **anotar**
To loiter - **holgazanear**
To loll - **recostarse**
To long for - **anhelar**
To look - **mirar** 64
To look after - **cuidar** 26
To look for - **buscar** 65
To look like - **parecer** 84
Look out! - **cuidado!**
To look out onto *(as a window)* - **dar a** 45
To loom - **aparecer** 84
To loop - **enlazar**
To loop the loop - **rizar el rizo**
To loosen - **aflojar**
To loot - **saquear**
To lop - **cortar**
To lose - **perder** 66
To lounge - **holgazanear**
To love - **amar**
To lower - **bajar**
To lubricate - **lubrificar**
To lull - **arrullar**
To lunch - **almorzar**
To lurch - **tambalear**
To lure - **tentar**
To lurk - **acechar**
To lust - **codiciar**
To luxuriate - **vivir lujosamente** 63
To lynch - **linchar**

M

To madden - **enloquecer**
To magnify *(optically)* - **magnificar**
To magnify *(generally)* - **aumentar**
To mail - **mandar por correo** 86
To maim - **mutilar**
To maintain - **mantener**
To make - **hacer** 32
To make a mistake - **equivocar**
To make an appointment - **citar**
To make a payment - **efectuar un pago**
To make money - **ganar dinero**
To make sense - **tener sentido**
To malign - **difamar**
To maltreat - **maltratar**
To manacle - **maniatar**
To manage - **manejar**
To mangle - **mutilar**
To manicure - **cuidar las manos** 26
To manifest - **manifestar**
To manipulate - **manipular**
To manoeuver - **maniobrar**
To manufacture - **manufacturar**
To map out - **proyectar**
To mar - **estropiar**
To march - **marchar** 58
To mark - **marcar**
To market - **vender** 85
To maroon - **abandonar**
To marry - **casar**
To marshall - **ordenar**
To marvel - **maravillarse**
To mash - **triturar**
To mask - **enmascarar**
To masquerade - **enmascararse**
To mass together - **juntar**
To masacre - **masacrar**
To massage - **dar masaje**
To master - **dominar**
To mat together - **enredar**
To match - **aparear**
To match *(compete with)* - **competir con**
To mate - **emparejar**
To matriculate - **matricular**
To matter - **tener importancia**
It does not matter - **no importa**
What's the matter? - **que pasa?**
To mature - **madurar**
To maul - **apalear**
May *(to be able)* - **poder** 19
I may be *(something)* - **puedo ser** 9
I may be *(somewhere)* - **puedo estar** 9
It may be - **puede ser** 9
I may go - **puedo ir** 19/46
May I come in? - **puedo entrar?** 19/37

M (cont.)

See Page

You may go! - **puede usted marcharse!**
To mean - **significar**
I mean - **quiero decir** 106/82
To mean to - **intentar** 101
What does this mean? - **qué significa esto?**
What do you mean? - **qué quieres decir?**
To meander - **vagar**
To measure - **medir**
To mechanize - **mecanizar**
To meddle - **entrometerse**
To mediate - **mediar**
To meditate - **meditar**
To meet *(encounter)* - **encontrar** 40
To meet someone - **hallar** 67
To meet together as a group - **juntar** *or* - **reunir**
To mellow - **madurar**
To melt - **disolver**
To memorize - **memorizar**
To menace - **amenazar**
To mend - **reparar**
To menstruate - **menstruar**
To mention - **mencionar**
To merge - **unir**
To merit - **merecer**
To merry make - **hacer fiesta**
To mesh - **enredar**
To mess *(feed)* - **dar de comer** 45/35
To make a mess - **ensuciar**
To mess up *(disarrange)* - **desordenar**
To meter - **medir**
To mew - **maullar**
Might *(to be able)* - **poder** 19
To migrate - **emigrar**
To mildew - **enmohecer**
To milk - **ordeñar**
To mill - **moler**
To mime - **imitar**
To mince - **desmenuzar**
To mind - **tener cuidado** 50/26
To mine - **minar**
To mingle - **mezclar**
To minimize - **reducir al minimo**
To minister - **administar**
To mint *(coins)* - **acuñar**
To mirror - **reflejar**
To misapply - **aplicar mal**
To misapprehend - **entender mal** 102
To misbehave - **portarse mal**
To miscalculate - **calcular mal**

See Page

To miscarry - **fracasar**
To misconceive - **juzgar mal**
To misconduct - **conducir mal** 34
To miscount - **contar mal** 30
To misfire - **fallar un tiro**
To misguide - **dirigir mal**
To misinform - **informar mal**
To misinterpret - **interpretar mal**
To misjudge - **juzgar mal**
To mislay - **perder** 66
To mislead - **engañar**
To mismanage - **administrar mal**
To misplace - **colocar mal**
To misprint - **imprimar mal**
To mispronounce - **pronunciar mal**
To misrepresent - **tergiversar**
To miss *(trains etc.)* - **perder** 66
To be missing - **faltar**
To miss out - **omitir**
To misspell - **deletrear mal**
To mist - **obscurecer**
To mistake - **equivocar**
And no mistake - **sin falta**
By mistake - **por descuido**
To make a mistake - **equivocar**
To mistrust - **desconfiar**
To misunderstand - **entender mal** 102
To misuse - **usar mal** 103
To mitigate - **mitigar**
To mix - **mezclar**
To moan - **lamentar**
To moan *or* groan - **gemir**
To moan *or* complain - **protestar**
To mob - **atropellar**
To mobilize - **movilizar**
To mock - **burlar**
To model - **modelar**
To moderate - **moderar**
To modernize - **modernizar**
To modify - **modificar**
To modulate - **modular**
To moisten - **humedecer**
To mold *(go mouldy)* - **enmohecer**
To molest - **molestar**
To monitor - **controlar**
To monopolize - **monopolizar**
To moo - **mugir**
To moor *(as a boat)* - **amarrar**
To mop - **fregar**
To mope - **preocupar**
To moralize - **moralizar**
To mortgage - **hipotecar**
To mortify - **mortificar**

M (cont.)

	See Page
To mother - **servir de madre a**	
To motivate - **motivar**	
To motorize - **motorizar**	
To mottle - **motear**	
To mould *or* shape - **moldear**	
To mould *(go mouldy)* - **enmohecer**	
To mount - **montar**	
To mour - **lamentar**	
To move - **mover**	68
To move along - **caminar**	
To move aside - **apartar**	
To move away - **marchar**	58
To move down - **bajar**	
To move forward - **adelantar**	
To move in - **entrar**	37
To move off - **marchar**	58
To move out - **salir**	48
To move up - **adelantar**	
To mow - **segar**	
To muddle - **desordenar**	
To muffle *(a sound)* - **amortiguar**	
To muffle *(as with a scarf)* - **embozar**	
To multiply - **multiplicar**	
To mumble - **refunfuñar**	
To mummify - **momificar**	
To munch - **mascar**	
To murder - **asesinar**	
To murmur - **murmurar**	
To "must" - **tener que**	51
To muster - **convocar**	
To mutilate - **mutilar**	
To mutiny - **amontinarse**	
To mutter - **refunfuñar**	
To muzzle - **abozalar**	
To mystify - **confundir**	

N

	See Page
To nag - **regañar**	
To nail - **clavar**	
To name - **nombrar**	
To be named - **llamarse**	25
To nap *(have one)* - **sestear**	
To narrate - **narrar**	
To narrow - **estrechar**	
To naturalize - **naturalizar**	
To nauseate - **nausear**	
To navigate - **navegar**	
To near - **acercar**	
To necessitate - **necesitar**	69
To need - **necesitar**	69
To negate - **negar**	
To neglect - **descuidar**	26
To negotiate - **negociar**	
To neigh - **relinchar**	
To nest - **anidar**	
To nestle - **acurrucar**	
To net - **enredar**	
To nett *(business)* - **producir**	
To nibble - **roer**	
To nick *or* notch - **cortar**	
To nip - **pellizcar**	
To nod - **cabecear**	
To nominate - **nombrar**	
To notch - **cortar mellas**	
To note - **anotar**	
To notice - **observar**	
To notify - **notificar**	
To nourish - **nutrir**	
To nudge - **dar un codazo**	
To number - **numerar**	
To nurse - **cuidar**	26
To nurture - **criar**	

O

	See Page
To obey - **obedecer**	
To object - **objetar**	
To obligate - **obligar**	
To oblige - **obligar**	
To obliterate - **obliterar**	
To obscure - **obscurecer**	
To observe -**observar**	
To obsess - **obsesionar**	
To obstruct - **obstruir**	
To obtain - **obtener**	
To obtain *(get)* - **conseguir**	44
To obtrude - **imponer**	
To obviate - **obviar**	
To occasion - **ocasionar**	
To occupy - **ocupar**	
To occur - **ocurrir**	
To offend - **ofender**	
To offer - **ofrecer**	
To officiate - **oficiar**	
To offset - **compensar**	
To oil - **lubricar**	
To omit - **omitir**	
To ooze - **exudar**	
To open - **abrir**	70
To operate - **operar**	
To oppose - **oponer**	
To oppress - **oprimir**	
To opt - **optar**	
To orbit - **dar vueltas en órbita**	
To ordain - **ordenar**	
To order - **ordenar**	
To order *(as a meal)* - **pedir**	16

O (cont.)

	See Page
To organize - **organizar**	
To orientate - **orientar**	
To originate - **originar**	
To oscillate - **oscilar**	
Ought - **deber**	**71**
To oust - **desalojar**	
To out - **expeler**	
To outbid - **sobrepujar**	
To outclass - **exceder**	
To outdate - **anticuar**	
To outdo - **sobrepujar**	
To outfit - **equipar**	
To outlast - **durar más que**	
To outlaw - **proscribir**	
To outlay - **desembolsar**	
To outlive - **sobrevivir**	**63**
To outnumber - **exceder en numero**	
To outrage - **ultrajar**	
To outroot - **desarraigar**	
To outrun - **correr más que otra**	
To outshine - **eclipsar**	
To outstrech - **extender**	
To outweigh - **pesar más que**	
To outwit - **ser más listo**	
To outwear - **durar más tiempo que**	
To over act - **exagerar**	
To overbalance - **perder el equilibrio**	
To overbear - **oprimir**	
To overburden - **sobrecargar**	
To overcharge - **sobrecargar**	
To overcome - **superar**	
To overdo - **exceder**	
To overdraw - **sobregirar**	
To overeat - **comer demasiado**	**35**
To overflow - **inundar**	
To overhang - **colgar por encima de**	
To overhaul - **revisar**	
To overhear - **alcanzar a oír**	
To overheat - **calentar con exceso**	
To overload - **sobrecargar**	
To overlook *(miss)* - **faltar**	
To overlook *(look over)* - **mirar por encima**	**64**
To overlook *(as a window etc.)* - **dar a**	**45**
To overlap - **solapar**	
To overpower - **subyugar**	
To override - **anular**	
To overrate - **sobreestimar**	
To overrun - **invadir**	
To oversee - **vigilar**	
To overstate - **exagerar**	
To overstock - **abarrotar**	
To overtake - **alcanzar**	
To overtax - **sobrecargar de impuestos**	
To overtax *(oneself)* - **cansarse**	
To overthrow - **derrocar**	
To overturn - **volcar**	
To overwhelm - **abrumar**	
To overwork - **trabajar demasiado**	**109**
To owe - **deber**	**71**
To own - **poseer**	

P

	See Page
To pace *(measure time)* - **medir a pasos**	
To pace (as up & down etc.) - **pasear**	
To pace oneself - **controlarse**	
To pacify - **pacificar**	
To package *or* pack - **embolar**	
To pack *(suitcase)* - **hacer una maleta**	**32**
To be packed in *(like sardines)* - **estar apretados como sardinas en lata!**	
To pack *or* cram - **abarrotar**	
To pack up *(finish)* - **terminar**	**41**
To packet - **empacar**	
To pad - **almohadillar**	
To paddle - **chapotear**	
To padlock - **cerrar con candado**	**28**
To be in pain - **doler**	**10**
To paint - **pintar**	
To pair - **aparear**	
To pale - **palidecer**	
To palm - **cubrir con palmas**	
To palm off - **engañar**	
To palpitate - **palpitar**	
To pamper - **mimar**	
To pander - **alcahuetear**	
To panic - **tener pánico**	**50**
To pant - **jadear**	
To parachute - **lanzar en paracaídas**	
To parade - **cabalgar**	
To paralyse - **paralizar**	
To parcel - **parcelar**	
To parch - **tostar**	
To pardon - **perdonar**	
To pare - **recortar**	
To park *(a car)* - **aparcar**	
To parody - **parodiar**	
To parry - **parar**	**91**
To part - **partir**	
To partake - **participar**	
To participate - **participar**	
To partition - **dividir**	

P (cont.)

See Page

To partner - **acompañar**
To pas - **pasar**
To paste *or* stick - **pegar**
To pasteurize - **pasterizar**
To pat - **acariciar**
To patch - **remendar**
To patent - **patentar**
To be patient - **estar paciente** **18**
To patrol - **rondar**
To patronize *(as a restaurant etc.)* - **favorecer**
To pattern - **copiar**
To pause - **parar** **91**
To pave - **pavimentar**

To paw *or* fondle - **acariciar**
To the ground - **dar zarpazos**
To pawn - **empeñar**
To pay - **pagar** **72**
To pay back - **reembolsar**
To pay in cash - **pagar al contado** **72**
To pay out - **desembolsar**
To pay a visit - **hacer una visita** **32**
To peak - **subir al pico**
To peck - **picotear**
To pedal - **pedalear**
To peddle - **vender por las calles** **85**

To peek *or* peep - **atisbar**
To peel - **pelar**
To peer - **escudriñar**
To peg - **clavar**
To pelt - **golpear** **53**
To pelt down - **caer con fuerza** **38**
To pen - **escribir** **110**
To pencil - **escribir con lapiz**
To be pending - **estar pendiente**
To penetrate - **penetrar**
To pension - **pensionar**
To pep up - **dar ánimo** **45**
To pepper *(pierce with holes)* - **acribillar**
To pepper *(season)* - **sazonar con pimienta**
To perceive - **percibir**
To perch - **emperchar**
To percolate - **infiltrar**
To perfect - **perfeccionar**
To perforate - **perforar**
To perform - **actuar**
To perfume - **perfumar**
To perish - **perecer**

See Page

To perjure - **perjurar**
To permeate - **penetrar**
To permit - **permitir**
To pepetrate - **perpetrar**
To perpetuate - **perpetuar**
To perplex - **confundir**
To persecute - **perseguir**
To persevere - **perseverar**
To persist - **persistir**
To personalize - **personalizar**
To personify - **personificar**
To perspire - **sudar**
To persuade - **persuadir**
To pertain - **pertenecer**
To perturb - **perturbar**
To peruse - **leer con cuidado** **79/26**
To pervade- **penetrar**
To pervert - **pervertir**
To pester - **molestar**
To pet - **mimar**
To petition - **suplicar**
To phase - **poner en fase** **77**
To philosophize - **filosofar**
To phone - **telefonear**
To photograph - **fotografiar**
To phrase - **frasear**
To pick - **picar**
To pick *or* choose - **seleccionar**
To pick up - **recoger**
To picket - **estar de guardia** **18**
To pickle - **escabechar**
To pinic - **merender en el campo**
To picture *(draw one)* - **dibujar**
To picture *(paint one)* - **pintar**
To picture - **imaginar**
To pierce - **penetrar**
To pile up - **amontonar**
To pilfer - **ratear**
To pillage - **saquear**
To pilot - **pilotar**
To pin - **prender con alfileres**
To pinch - **pellizcar**
To pine - **anhelar**
To pioneer - **explorar**
To pity - **compadecer**
To pivot - **pivotar**
To place - **poner** **77**
To plague - **plagar**
To plait - **trenzar**
To plan - **planear**
To plane *or* glide - **planear**
To plane *(wood)* - **garlopar**
To plant - **plantar**

P (cont.)

See Page

To plaster - **enyesar**
To plate - **platear**
To play - **jugar** **73**
To play *(musical instrument)* - **tocar** **98**
To plead *(against)* - **abogar**
To plead with - **suplicar**
To please - **agradar**
To be pleasing to - **gustar** **60**
To pleat - **plegar**

To pledge - **prometer**
To plod - **andar dificultosamente** **105**
To plot - **conspirar**
To plough - **arar**
To pluck - **arrancar**
To plug - **tapar**
To plumb *(the depths)* - **sondear**
To plumb *(as a plumber would)* - **instalar cañerias**
To plunder - **saquear**
To plunge - **zambullir**
To ply - **ejercer**
To ply between - **hacer el servicio entre** **32**
To ply with questions - **preguntar** **15**
To poach *(eggs etc.)* - **escalfar**
To poach *(as a poacher)* - **cazar *or* pescar furtivamente**
To pocket - **embolsar**
To point - **apuntar**
To point to - **indicar**
To point out - **enseñar** **96**
To poison - **envenenar**
To poke - **atizar**
To polish - **pulir**
To poll - **votar**
To pollute - **contaminar**
To ponder - **ponderar**
To pop - **hacer pum!** **32**
To pop in - **entrar de repente** **37**
To pop out - **salir de repente** **48**
To popularize - **popularizar**
To populate - **poblar**
To pore over - **estudiar con atención**
To portray - **retratar**
To pose *(as a model)* - **posar**
To pose as *or* show off - **alardear**
To pose problems *or* questions - **confundir con preguntas o dificultades**
To position - **colocar**

See Page

To possess - **poseer**
To post *or* station - **apostar**
To post a letter - **mandar por correo** **86**
To postpone - **posponer**
To pot *(fruit etc.)* - **conservar**
To pot *(plants)* - **plantar en macetas**
To pounce - **abalanzar**
To pound - **golpear a menudo** **53**
To pour - **echar** **74**
To pout - **hacer pucheros** **32**
To powder - **empolvar**
To power - **impulsar**
To practise - **practicar**
To praise - **alabar**
To prance - **cabriolar**
To pray - **orar**
To preach - **sermonear**
To precede - **preceder**
To precipitate - **precipitar**
To preclude - **excluir**
To predestine - **predestinar**
To predict - **predecir**
To predispose - **predisponer**
To predominate - **predominar**
To prefer - **preferir** **75**
To prefix - **prefijar**
To prejudge - **prejuzgar**
To prejudice - **predisponer**
To premeditate - **premeditar**
To preoccupy - **preocupar**
To prepar - **preparar**
To prepay - **pagar por adelantado** **72**
To prescribe - **prescribir**
To present - **presentar**
To preserve - **conservar**
To preside - **presidir**
To press - **prensar**
To press *(clothes etc.)* - **planchar**
To pressurize - **sobrecargar**
To presume - **presumir**
To presuppose - **presuponer** **92**
To pretend - **pretender**
To prevail - **prevalecer**
To prevent - **prevenir**
To prey upon - **pillar**
To price - **evaluar**
To prick - **pinchar**
To prime - **preparar**
To print - **imprimir**
To privilege - **privilegiar**
To prize - **apreciar**
To probe - **sondear**

P (cont.)

See Page

To proceed - **seguir** 47
To process - **procesar**
To proclaim - **proclamar**
To procreate - **procrear**
To procure - **procurar**
To prod - **punzar**
To produce - **producir**
To profess - **profesar**
To profit by - **aprovechar**
To prognosticate - **pronosticar**
To progress - **progresar**
To prohibit - **prohibir**
To project - **proyectar**
To prolong - **prolongar**
To promenade - **pasear**
To promise - **prometer**
To promote - **promocionar**
To prompt - **sugerir**
To promulgate - **promulgar**
To pronounce - **pronunciar**
To prop up - **apuntalar**
To propagate - **propagar**
To propel - **impeler**
To prophesy - **profetizar**
To proportion - **proporcionar**
To propose - **proponer**
To proscribe - **proscribir**
To prosecute - **acusar**
To prospect - **explorar**
To propser - **prosperar**
To prostitute - **prostituir**
To prostrate - **postrar**
To protect - **proteger**
To protest - **protestar**
To protract - **prolongar**
To protrude - **sobresalir** 48
To prove - **sustanciar**
To provide - **proveer** 76
To provoke - **provocar**
To prowl - **andar al acecho** 105
To prune - **podar**
To pry *or* spy - **espiar**
To pry into - **fisgar**
To pry open - **forzar**
To psychoanalyze - **sicoanalizar**
To publish - **publicar**
To publisize - **advertir**
To pucker - **fruncir**
To puff *or* blow - **soplar**
To puff and blow - **jadear**
To pull - **arrastrar**
To pull apart *or* asunder - **arrancar**
To pull back - **cejar**

See Page

To pull down - **demoler**
To pull something in - **tirar hacia dentro**
To pull in *(as in a train to a station)* - **entrar** 37
To pull out - **salir** 48
To pull something up - **levantar**
To pull up *or* stop - **parar** 91
To pulsate - **pulsar**
To pulverize - **pulverizar**
To pump - **bombear**
To pump up - **inflar**
To punch - **punzar**
To punctuate - **puntuar**
To puncture - **pinchar**
To punish - **castigar**
To purchase - **comprar** 23
To purge - **purgar**
To purify - **purificar**
To purport - **significar**
To purr - **ronronear**
To pursue - **seguir** 47
To push - **empujar**
To push away - **rechazar**
To push in *(dent)* - **meter**
To push in - **introducir**
To push in *(into a queue)* - **introducirse a codazos**
To push off *(as a boat)* - **desatracar**
To push out - **expulsar**
To push through - **forzar**
To put - **poner** 77
To put aside - **rechazar**
To put something away - **guardar**
To put back *or* replace - **reponer** 77
To put back *or* retard - **retardar**
To put back *or* return - **volver** 81
To put something down - **dejar** 59
To put forward - **proponer**
To put in - **introducir**
To put into port - **arribar**
To put off - **posponer**
To put on *(clothes etc.)* - **ponerse** 78
To put something out - **expeler**
To put out *or* extinguish - **extinguir**
To put out *or* depart - **salir** 48
To put to bed - **acostar**
To put together *or* join - **acoplar**
To put together *or* gather - **acumular**
To put to sea - **hacerse a la mar**
To put to use - **usar** 103
To put up *or* erect - **construir**
To put up *or* accommodate - **hospedar**

See Page

To put up with - **tolerar**
To putrify - **pudrir**
To puzzle - **confundir**

Q

To quack - **parpar**
To quaff - **beber a grandes tragos** 33
To quake - **temblar**
To qualify - **calificar**
To quaranteen - **poner en cuarentena** 77
To quarrel - **altercar**
To quarter *(cut in four)* - **cuarterar**
To quarter *(house)* - **hospedar**
To quash - **anular**
To quaver - **temblar**
To quell - **sujetar**
To quench *(a fire)* - **extinguir**
To quench *(one's thirst)* - **satisfacer**
To query - **preguntar** 15
To question - **preguntar** 15
To queue - **hacer cola** 32
To quicken - **acelerar**
To quieten - **acquietar**
To quilt - **alcolchar**
To quit - **abandonar**
To quiver - **temblar**
To quiz - **interrogar**
To quote - **citar**

R

To race - **competir**
To racketeer - **extorsionar**
To radiate - **radiar**
To raffle - **sortear**
To rage - **rabiar**
To raid - **atacar**
To rain - **llover**
To raise - **levantar**
To rake - **rastrillar**
To rally - **reunir**
To ram - **atacar**
To ramble - **pasear**
To ranch - **dirigir un rancho**
To range over - **recorrer**
To rank *or* rate - **evaluar**
To rank over - **tener grado superior** 50
To ransack - **saquear**
To ransom - **rescatar**
To rant - **gritar**
To rape - **violar**

See Page

To rasp - **raspar**
To rate - **evaluar**
To ratify - **ratificar**
To ration - **racionar**
To rationalize - **racionalizar**
To rattle *(make a noise)* - **hacer ruido** 32
To rattle *or* confuse - **confundir**
To ravage - **saquear**
To rave - **disparatar**
To rave about someone - **estar loco por** 18
To ravish - **violar**
To raze - **demoler**
To reach - **alcanzar**
To react - **reaccionar**
To read - **leer** 79
To readjust - **reajustar**
To be ready - **disponerse**
To make ready - **preperar**
To re-affirm - **reafirmar**
To realize - **realizar**
To reap - **cosechar**
To reappear - **reaparecer** 84
To rear - **cultivar**
To rear up - **elevar**
To rear up *(as a horse)* - **encabritarse**
To reason - **razonar**
To reassemble - **reunir**
To reassure - **reasegurar**
To rebel - **rebelarse**
To rebound - **rebotar**
To rebuff - **rechazar**
To rebuild - **reconstruir**
To rebuke - **reprender**
To recall *or* remember - **recordar** 80
To recall *or* retract - **retractar**
To recapture - **recapturar**
To recast - **reconstruir**
To recede - **retroceder**
To receive - **recibir**
To reciprocate - **reciprocar**
To recite - **recitar**
To reckon - **calcular**
To reclaim - **reclamar**
To recline - **reclinar**
To recognize - **reconocer** 56
To recoil - **recular**
To recollect - **recordar** 80
To recommend - **recomendar**
To recompense - **recompensar**
To reconcile - **reconciliar**
To reconnoitre - **explorar**

R (cont.)

	See Page
To reconsider - **reconsiderar**	
To reconstruct - **reconstruir**	
To record - **recordar**	**80**
To record *(on file)* - **archivar**	
To record *(on tape)* - **grabar en cinta magnetofónica**	
To recount - **recontar**	**30**
To recover *(get back)* - **recobrar**	
To recover *(get well)* - **recuperar**	
To recreate - **recrear**	
To recruit - **reclutar**	
To rectify - **rectificar**	
To recuperate - **recuperar**	
To recur - **repetir**	
To redden - **ruborizarse**	
To redeem - **redimir**	
To redouble - **redoblar**	
To redress - **rectificar**	
To reduce - **reducir**	
To reek - **ahumar**	
To re-elect - **reelegir**	
To reenforce - **reforzar**	
To re-establish - **restablecer**	
To refer - **referir**	
To refill - **rellenar**	
To refine - **refinar**	
To refit - **restaurar**	
To reflect - **reflectar**	
To reform - **reformar**	
To refrain - **refrener**	
To refresh - **refrescar**	
To refrigerate - **refrigerar**	
To refund - **reembolsar**	
To refuse - **negar**	
To refute - **refutar**	
To regain - **recobrar**	
To regard - **considerar**	
To regenerate - **regenerar**	
To register - **registrar**	
To regret - **sentir**	**39**
To regulate - **arreglar**	**13**
To rehabilitate - **rehabilitar**	
To rehearse - **ensayar**	
To reign - **reinar**	
To reimburse - **reembolsar**	
To reinforce - **reforzar**	
To reinstate - **restablecer**	
To reject - **rechazar**	
To rejoice - **alegrar**	
To rejoin - **reunir**	
To rejuvenate - **rejuvenecer**	
To relapse - **recaer**	**38**
To relate to - **relatar**	
To relate *or* tell - **contar**	**30**
To relax - **relajar**	
To relay - **transmitir**	
To release - **soltar**	
To relent - **aplacar**	
To relieve - **relevar**	
To relish - **saborear**	
To rely on - **confiar en**	
To remain - **permanecer**	**90**
To remake - **rehacer**	**32**
To remark upon - **comentar**	
To remedy - **remediar**	
To remember - **recordar**	**80**
To remind - **recordar**	**80**
To reminisce - **pensar *or* hablar del pasado**	**97 / 89**
To remit - **remitir**	
To remodel - **remodelar**	
To remonstrate - **protestar**	
To remove - **remover**	**68**
To remunerate - **remunerar**	
To rend - **arrancar**	
To render - **dar**	**45**
To renew - **renovar**	
To renounce - **renunciar**	
To renovate - **renovar**	
To rent - **arrendar**	
To reopen - **reabrir**	**70**
To repair - **reparar**	
To repay - **reembolsar**	
To repeal - **revocar**	
To repeat - **repitir**	
To repel - **repeler**	
To repent - **arrepentirse**	
To repercuss - **repercutir**	
To replace- **reponer**	**77**
To replensih - **rellenar**	
To reply - **contestar**	**12**
To report - **informar**	
To repose - **descansar**	
To reprehend - **reprender**	
To represent - **representar**	
To repress - **reprimir**	
To reprieve - **aliviar**	
To reprimand - **reprender**	
To reprint - **reimprimir**	
To reproach - **reprochar**	
To reproduce - **reproducir**	
To reprove - **reprochar**	
To repudiate - **repudiar**	
To repulse - **repulsar**	
To repute - **reputar**	
To request - **pedir**	**16**

R (cont.)

	See Page
To require - **requerir**	
To requisition - **demandar**	
To rescind - **rescindir**	
To rescue - **rescatar**	
To research - **investigar**	
To resemble - **parecerse a**	**84**
To resent - **resentirse**	
To reserve - **reservar**	
To reside - **residir**	
To resign - **resignar**	
To resist - **resistir**	
To resolve - **acordar**	
To resound - **resonar**	
To respect - **respetar**	
To respire - **respirar**	
To respond - **responder**	
To rest - **descansar**	
To restore - **restituir**	
To restrain - **represar**	
To restrict - **limitar**	
To result - **resultar**	
To resume - **reasumir**	
To resume negotiations - **volver a tratar**	**81**
To resurrect - **resucitar**	
To retail - **vender**	**85**
To retain - **retener**	**54**
To retaliate - **desquitarse**	
To retard - **retardar**	
To retire - **retirar**	
To retire to bed - **acostarse**	
To retouch - **retocar**	**98**
To retrace - **repasar**	
To retract - **retractar**	
To retreat - **retirarse**	
To retrench - **atrincherar**	
To retrive - **recobrar**	
To return - **volver**	**81**
To reunite - **reunir**	
To reveal - **revelar**	
To revel in - **gozarse en**	**36**
To revenge - **vengar**	
To revere - **venerar**	
To reverse - **invertir**	
To revert - **retroceder**	
To review - **revistar**	
To revile - **denigrar**	
To revise - **revisar**	
To revive - **resucitar**	
To revoke - **revocar**	
To revolt - **rebelar**	
To revolutionize - **revolucionar**	
To revolve - **girar**	

	See Page
To reward - **premiar**	
To rewrite - **volver a escribir**	**81**
To rhyme - **rimar**	
To rid - **librar**	
To riddle *(with holes)* - **acribilar**	
To ride - **montar**	
To ride *(a bicycle)* - **ir en bicicleta**	**46**
To ride *(a horse)* - **cabalgar**	
To ride *(in a car or coach)* - **pasear en coche**	
To ridicule - **ridiculizar**	
To rifle - **robar**	
To rig out - **equipar**	
To rig up - **hacer**	**32**
To right - **rectificar**	
To ring *(encircle)* - **circundar**	
To ring *(as a bell)* - **sonar**	
To ring a door bell - **tocar el timbre**	**98**
To ring *(phone)* - **telefonear**	
To rinse - **lavar**	**107**
To riot - **alborotar**	
To rip - **rasgar**	
To ripen - **madurar**	
To ripple - **rizar**	
To rise - **subir**	
To risk - **arriesgar**	
To rival - **revalizar**	
To rivet - **remachar**	
To roam - **vagar**	
To roar - **rugir**	
To roast - **asar**	
To rob - **robar**	
To rock - **arrullar**	
To roll - **rodar**	
To romp - **brincar**	
To roof - **techar**	
To be rooted - **raizar**	
To root out - **desarraigar**	
To rot - **pudrir**	
To rotate - **girar**	
To roughen - **poner áspero**	**77**
To round off - **rodondear**	
To round up - **congregar**	
To rouse - **despertar**	
To rouse *or* excite - **excitar**	
To rout - **derrotar**	
To route - **encaminar**	
To rove - **vagar**	
To row *(a boat)* - **remar**	
To row *or* argue - **arguir**	
To rub - **frotar**	

R (cont.)

See Page

To rub out - **borrar**
To rue - **lamentar**
To ruffle - **agitar**
To ruin - **arruinar**
To rule - **gobernar**
To rule out - **descartar**
To rumble - **retumbar**
To ruminate - **rumiar**
To rummage - **escudriñar**
To rumour - **rumorear**
To rumple - **arrugar**
To run - **correr**
To run away - **escapar**
To run *(as an engine etc.)* - **marchar** **58**
To run out of something - **quedar sin.**
To rupture - **romper**
To rush - **arrojar**
To rust - **oxidar**
To rustle - **susurrar**

S

To sabotage - **sabotear**
To sack *(put in one)* - **ensacar**
To sack *(an employee)* - **despedir**
To sacrifice - **sacrificar**
To sadden - **enstristecer**
To saddle - **ensillar**
To safeguard - **guardar**
To sag - **combar**
To sail - **navegar**
To salt - **salar**
To salute - **saludar**
To salvage - **salvar**
To sample - **probar** **95**
To sanction - **sancionar**
To put sand - **enarenar**
To sand down - **pulir**
To sandpaper - **pulir**
To sandwich - **intercalar**
To sap - **zapar**
To sate *or* satiate - **saciar**
To satirize - **satirizar**
To satisfy - **satisfacer**
To saturate - **saturar**
To saunter - **pasear**
To save from - **salvar**
To save *(conserve)* - **conservar**
To save *(money etc.)* - **ahorrar**
To save a place - **reservar**
To savour - **saborear**
To saw - **serrar**
To say - **decir** **82**

See Page

To scald - **escaldar**
To scale *or* climb - **escalar**
To scale down - **reducir**
To scalp - **escalpar**
To scamper *or* scarper - **escapar**
To scan - **mirar** **64**
To scandalize - **escandalizar**
To scar - **cicatrizar**
To scare - **asustrar**
To scatter - **dispersar**
To scent *(to be able to)* - **oler**
To scent *(put purfume)* - **perfumar**
To schedule - **catalogar**
To scheme - **planear**
To school - **enseñar** **96**
To scintillate - **centellear**
To scoff - **burlar**
To scold - **reprender**
To scoop out - **excavar**
To scoot - **correr**
To scoot *(on a child's scooter)* - **correr en patinete**
To scorch - **chamuscar**
To score *or* scratch - **rayar**
To score points - **ganar tantos**
To scourn - **despreciar**
To scour *or* scrub - **fregar**
To scour *or* look for - **buscar** **65**
To scourge *or* flog - **azotar**
To scout - **explorar**
To scowl - **mirar con ceño** **64**
To scramble up *or* climb - **trepar**
To scramble up *or* mix - **mezclar**
To scramble *(eggs)* - **cocinar huevos revueltos**
To scrap - **descartar**
To scrape - **raspar**
To scratch - **rayar**
To scratch oneself - **arañarse**
To scrawl - **garabatear**
To scream *or* screech - **chillar**
To screen *or* protect - **proteger**
To screen from view - **ocultar**
To screen *(a film)* - **cinematografiar**
To screw - **atornillar**
To scribble - **garabatear**
To scrub - **fregar**
To scrunch - **ronzar**
To scrutinize - **escrutar**
To scuffle - **pelear**
To sculpt - **esculpir**
To scurry - **escabullir**
To scuttle *(a ship)* - **barrenar**

S (cont.)

See Page

To scythe - **guadañar**
To seal - **sellar**
To seam - **coser**
To search - **buscar** **65**
To season - **sazonar**
To seat - **sentar**
To seat oneself - **sentarse** **87**
To second *or* support - **apoyar**
To secrete *or* hide - **esconder**
To secrete *or* ooze - **exudar**
To section - **seccionar**
To secure - **asegurar**
To sedate - **sedar**
To seduce - **seducir**
To see - **ver** **83**
To seed - **sembrar**
To seek - **buscar** **65**
To seem - **parecer** **84**
To seep - **filtrar**
To seethe - **hervir**
To segment - **dividir en segmentos**
To segregate - **segregar**
To seize - **coger**
To seize *(judicially)* - **embargar**
To select - **seleccionar**
To sell - **vender** **85**
To send - **mandar** **86**
To sense - **sentir** **39**
To sentence - **sentenciar**
To separate - **separar**
To serenade - **dar una serenata**
To serve - **servir**
To service - **mantener**
To set - **poner** **77**
To set aside - **poner un lado** **77**
To set fire to - **encender**
To set free - **liberar**
To set off - **salir** **48**
To set sail - **zarpar**
To set up - **establecer**
To settle - **asentar**
To settle down - **calmar**
To settle for - **seleccionar**
To settle upon - **decidir**
To sever - **cortar**
To sew - **coser**
To shackle - **encadenar**
To shade - **sombrear**
To shake - **agitar**
To shake hands - **estrechar las manos**
To shake off - **desechar**
To sham - **fingir**
To shamble - **andar bamboleándose** **105**

See Page

To shame - **avergonzar**
To shampoo - **lavar** **107**
To shape - **formar**
To share - **compartir**
To share out - **repartir**
To sharpen - **afilar**
To shatter - **fragmentar**
To shave *(one's beard)* - **afeitarse**
To shave *(wood etc.)* - **cepillar**
To shear - **esquilar**
To sheathe - **envainar**
To shed - **derramar**
To shell - **descascarar**
To shelter - **abrigar**
To shelve - **diferir**
To shepherd - **pastorear**
To shield - **escudar**
To shift - **mover** **68**
To shimmer - **rielar**
To shine - **brillar**
To ship - **embarcar**
To be shipwrecked - **naufragar**
To shirk - **eludir**
To shiver - **temblar**
To shock - **chocar**
To shoe - **calzar**
To shoot *(a gun)* - **disparar**
To shoot *(as a plant)* - **brotar**
To shoot at - **tirar a**
To shoot down - **derribar**
To shoot out - **lanzar**
To shoot up *(grow)* - **brotar**
To shop - **ir de tiendas** **46**
To shore up - **apuntalar**
To shorten - **acortar**
Should - **deber** **71**
To shoulder - **llevar a hombros** **27**
To shout - **gritar**
To shove - **empujar**
To shovel - **traspalar**
To show - **enseñar** **96**
To shower *(rain)* - **llover**
To shower *(take one)* - **duchar**
To shred - **desmenuzar**
To shriek - **chillar**
To shrink *or* shrivel - **encoger**
To shroud - **cubrir**
To shrug - **encogerse de hombros**
To shudder - **temblar**
To shuffle - **arrastrar los pies**
To shun - **esquivar**
To shut - **cerrar** **28**
To shut off *(supplies)* - **cortar**
To shut out - **excluir**

S (cont.)

See Page

To shut up - **encerrar** 28
Shut up! - **calla la boca!**
To be sick - **poner enfermo** 77
To sicken - **enfermar**
To side with - **tomar partido por** 93
To sieve *or* sift - **cribar**
To sigh - **suspirar**
To sight - **ver** 83
To sign one's name - **firmar**
To sign *or* signal - **señalar**
To signify - **significar**
To silence - **silenciar**
To simmer - **hervir a fuego lento**
To simplify - **simplificar**
To simulate - **simular**
To sin - **pecar**
To sing - **cantar**
To singe - **chamuscar**
To single out - **separar**
To sink - **hundir**
To sip - **sorber**
To siphon - **sacar con sifón** 94
To sire - **procrear**
To sit down - **sentarse** 87
To site - **colocar**
To be situated - **situar**
To size - **calibrar**
To sizzle - **chisporrotear**
To skate - **patinar**
To sketch - **diseñar**
To ski - **esquiar**
To skid - **patinar**
To skim along *or* over - **resbalar**
To skim *(milk)* - **desnatar**
To skimp - **economizar**
To skin - **pelar**
To skip - **brincar**
To skipper *(capatain a ship)* - **patronear**
To skirmish - **escaramuzar**
To skirt - **bordear**
To skylark - **juguetear**
To slacken - **aflojar**
To slam - **cerrar de golpe** 28/53
To slander - **difamar**
To slant - **inclinar**
To slap - **abofetear**
To slash - **acuchillar**
To slaughter *or* slay - **matar**
To sleep - **dormir** 88
To be sleepy - **tener sueño** 50
To sleet - **neviscar**
To sleigh - **ir en trinio** 46
To slice - **rebanar**

See Page

To slide - **deslizar**
To slim - **adelgazar**
To sling *(put something in one)* - **poner en cabestrillo** 77
To sling *or* hurl - **lanzar**
To slink - **andar furtivamente** 105
To slink away - **escabullir**
To slip - **deslizar**
To slip and fall - **tropezar**
To slip away - **escabullir**
To slip out - **salir** 48
To slip something out - **sacar** 94
To slit - **rajar**
To slobber - **babosear**
To slog - **trabajar duro** 109
To slop - **derramar**
To slope - **inclinar**
To slot into - **encajar**
To slow down - **reducir velocidad**
To be slow *(as a watch etc.)* - **retrasarse**
To sluice - **regar**
To slumber - **dormir** 88
To slump - **hundirse**
To smack - **golpear** 53
To smart - **escocer**
To smarten - **embellecer**
To smash - **romper**
To smear - **manchar**
To smell - **oler**
To have an odor - **tener olor** 50
To smell bad - **oler mal**
To smell good - **oler bien**
To smell of - **oler a**
To smell off - **husmear**
To smelt - **fundir**
To smile - **sonreir**
To smite - **golpear** 53
To smoke *(cigarettes etc.)* - **fumar**
To smoke *(salmon etc.)* - **ahumar**
To smooth - **suavizar**
To smother - **sofocar**
To smudge - **tiznar**
To smuggle - **contrabandear**
To snake - **serpentear**
To snap - **chasquear**
To snare - **atrapar con trampa**
To snarl - **gruñir**
To snatch - **arrebatar**
To sneak - **escabullir**
To sneer - **mofar**
To sneeze - **estornudar**
To sniff - **husmear**

S (cont.)

See Page

To snip - **recortar**
To snivel - **lloriquear**
To snoop - **fisgar**
To snooze - **sestear**
To snore - **roncar**
To snort - **resoplar**
To snow - **nevar**
To snub - **desdeñar**
To snuff out - **morir**
To soak - **empapar**
To soap - **enjabonar**
To soar - **elevarse**
To sob - **sollozar**
To sober up - **desemborrachar**
To socialize - **socializar**
To soften - **ablandar**
To soil - **ensuciar**
To solder - **soldar**
To sole *(shoes)* - **poner suelas** 77
To solicit - **solicitar**
To solidify - **solidificar**
To solve - **resolver**
To somersault - **dar una voltereta**
To soothe - **calmar**
To sophisticate - **sofisticar**
To sorrow - **afligirse**
To be sorry - **sentir** **39**
I am sorry - **lo siento** **39**
To sort - **clasificar**
To sound - **sonar**
To sour - **agriar**
To sow - **sembrar**
To space - **espaciar**
To span - **extenderse sobre**
To spank - **zurrar**
To spark - **centellear**
To sparkle - **chispear**
To spatter - **salpicar**
To speak - **hablar** **89**
To spear - **lanzear**
To specialize - **especializar**
To specify - **especificar**
To speckle - **manchar**
To speculate - **especular**
To speed - **ir a velocidad** **46**
To spell - **deletrear**
To spend *(money)* - **gastar**
To spend *(time)* - **pasar**
To spice - **sazonar**
To spike *or* spear - **lanzear**
To spill - **derramar**
To spin - **girar**
To spit - **escupir**

See Page

To spite - **mostrar resentimiento**
To splash - **salpicar**
To splice - **empalmar**
To splint - **entablillar**
To splinter - **entablillar**
To split - **dividir**
To splutter - **balbucear**
To spoil - **estropear**
To sponsor - **patrocinar**
To spoon out - **sacar con cuchara** **94**
To spot *(make spots)* - **manchar**
To spot *(notice)* - **notar**
To spout - **arrojar**
To sprain - **torcer**
To sprawl - **extenderse**
To spray - **rociar**
To spread - **extender**
To spread with - **cubrir con**
To spring - **brincar**
To sprinkle - **salpicar**
To sprint - **correr**
To sprout - **brotar**
To spruce up - **arreglarse** **13**
To spur - **espolear**
To spurn - **rechazar**
To spurt our - **salir rápidamente** **48**
To spurt *(run)* - **correr**
To spy - **espiar**
To squabble - **disputar**
To squander - **malgastar**
To make square - **cuadrar**
To squash - **aplastar**
To squat - **agacharse**
To squeak *or* squeal - **chillar**
To squeeze - **apretar**
To squeeze flat - **aplastar**
To squeeze in - **recalcar**
To squeeze out - **exprimir**
To squint - **mirar bizco** **64**
To squirm - **retorcerse**
To squirt - **arrojar a chorros**
To stab - **apuñalar**
To stabilize - **estabilizar**
To stable - **estabular**
To stack - **amontonar**
To staff - **proveer de personal** **76**
To stage - **escenificar**
To stagger *(about)* - **tambalear**
To stagger *(space out)* - **alternar**
To stagnate - **estancarse**
To stain - **manchar**
To stake out *or* fence - **estacar**
To stake *(wager)* - **arriesgar**

S (cont.)

See Page

To stalk - **cazar al acecho**
To stall *(as a horse)* -**encerrar** **28**
To stall *(as an engine)* - **parar** **91**
To stall for time - **posponer**
To stammer - **balbucir**
To stamp *(a letter)* - **sellar**
To stamp *(with rubber stamp)* - **estampar**
To stamp *(one's foot)* - **patear**
To stamp out - **eliminar**
To stampede - **huir**
To stand *or* place - **poner** **77**
To stand back - **quedarse atrás**
To stand for - **representar**
To stand on one's feet - **estar de pie** **18**
To stand out - **sobresalir** **48**
To stand up - **levantarse**
To stand up to - **resistir**
To standardize - **hacer uniforme** **32**
To staple - **grapar**
To star - **marcar con asterisco**
To star in - **presentarse en**
To starch - **almidonar**
To stare - **mirar fijamente** **64**
To start - **empezar** **20**
To start *(a car)* - **poner en marcha** **77/58**
To start *(a club or a business etc.)* - **fundar**
To start from - **salir de** **48**
To start to - **ponerse a** **78**
To startle - **alarmar**
To starve - **hambrear**
To starve to death - **morir de hambre**
To state - **declarar**
To station - **estacionar**
To staunch - **restañar**
To stave off - **diferir**
To stay - **permanecer** **90**
To stay at - **hospedarse**
To stay away - **no volver** **81**
To stay behind - **quedarse**
To stay in - **quedarse en casa**
To stay in bed - **guardar cama**
To stay out - **quedarse fuera**
To steady - **asegurar**
To steal - **robar**
To steam - **vaporizar**
To steam cook - **cocer al baño de Maria**
To steam up - **ocultar con vapor**
To steer - **gobernar**

See Page

To stem from - **provenir**
To stencil - **estarcir**
To step - **dar pasos** **45**
To step aside - **apartarse**
To step back - **retroceder**
To step down - **descencer**
To step inside - **entrar** **37**
To step on - **pisar**
To step outside - **salir** **48**
To step over - **atravesar**
To step up - **subir**
To sterilize - **esterilizar**
To stew - **estofar**
To stick - **pegar**
To stiffen - **reforzar**
To stifle - **sofocar**
To still - **calmar**
To stimulate - **estimular**
To sting - **picar**
To stink - **tener olor mal** **50**
To stint - **economizar**
To stipulate - **estipular**
To stir - **agitar**
To stitch - **coser**
To stock - **proveer** **76**
To stoke - **cargar**
To stone - **apedrear**
To stoop - **inclinarse**
To stop - **parar** **91**
To store - **guardar**
To storm - **asaltar**
To storm *(weather)* - **haber tormenta**
To stow - **guardar**
To stowaway - **embarcar clandestinamente**
To straddle - **ponerse a horcajadas** **78**
To straggle - **extraviarse**
To straighten - **enderezar**
To strain - **forzar**
To strangle - **estrangular**
To strap - **precintar**
To stray - **descarriarse**
To streak - **rayar**
To stream - **fluir**
To streamline - **aerodinamizar**
To strengthen - **reforzar**
To stress - **dar importancia** **45**
To stretch - **extender**
To strike - **golpear** **53**
To strike *(stop work)* - **declarar en huelga**
To strike at - **atacar**

S (cont.)

	See Page
To strike back - **contrarrestar**	
To strike down - **derribar**	
To strike out - **borrar**	
To strike a match - **encender un fósfero**	
To string - **encordar**	
To strop - **desnudar**	
To strip *(an engine)* - **desmontar**	
To strip *(for redecoration)* - **ordeñar completamente**	
To stripe - **rayar**	
To strive - **esforzarse**	
To stroke - **acariciar**	
To stroll - **pasear**	
To struggle - **luchar**	
To strut about - **farolear**	
To stud - **tachonar**	
To study - **estudiar**	
To stuff - **llenar**	
To stumble - **tropezar**	
To stun - **aturdir**	
To stupefy - **atontar**	
To stutter - **balbucir**	
To subdivide - **subdividir**	
To subdue - **subyugar**	
To subject - **sujetar**	
To subjugate - **subyugar**	
To sublet - **subarrendar**	
To submerge - **sumergir**	
To submit - **someter**	
To submit *(a proposition)* - **presentar**	
To submit *(a report)* - **rendir**	
To submit *(a suggestion)* - **hacer una sugestión**	**32**
To subscribe - **suscribir**	
To subside - **calmar**	
To substitute - **substituir**	
To subtract - **sustraer**	
To succeed *or* achieve - **conseguir**	**44**
To succeed *(in sequence)* - **suceder**	**49**
To succumb - **sucumbir**	
To suck - **chupar**	
To suck in - **embeber**	**33**
To suck out - **succionar**	
To suckle - **mamar**	
To sue - **demandar**	
To suffer - **sufrir**	
To suffer from - **padecer de**	
To suffice - **bastar**	
To suffocoate - **sofocar**	
To sugar - **azucarar**	
To suggest - **sugerir**	

	See Page
To suit - **satisfacer**	
To be suitable - **ser apropiado**	**17**
To sulk - **amurriarse**	
To sum up - **resumir**	
To summer - **veraniar**	
To summersault - **dar una voltereta**	
To summon - **citar**	
To sunbathe - **tomar el sol**	**93**
To be sunburnt - **tostado por el sol**	
To supervise - **supervisar**	
To supply - **proveer**	**76**
To support - **soportar**	
To suppose - **suponer**	**92**
To suppress - **suprimir**	
To be sure - **estar seguro**	**18**
To make sure - **asegurar**	
To surface - **subir a la superficie**	
To surmise - **suponer**	**92**
To surmount *or* surpass - **superar**	
To surprise - **sorprender**	
To surrender - **rendir**	
To surround - **circundar**	
To survey - **inspeccionar**	
To survive - **sobrevivir**	
To suspect - **sospechar**	
To suspend - **suspender**	
To sustain - **sostenar**	
To swab - **fregar**	
To swagger - **fanfarronear**	
To swallow - **tragar**	
To swamp - **inudar**	
To swap - **cambiar**	
To swarm - **enjambrar**	
To sway - **hacer oscilar**	**32**
To swear - **blasfemar**	
To swear at - **maldecir**	**82**
To swear in - **jurar**	
To swear off - **renunciar**	
To swear an oath - **juramentarse**	
To sweat - **sudar**	
To sweep - **barrer**	
To sweeten - **endulzar**	
To swell - **hinchar**	
To swelter - **sofocarse**	
To swill *or* hose down - **regar**	
To swim - **nadar**	
To swindle - **engañar**	
To swing - **columpiar**	
To swipe - **golpear**	**53**
To switch *or* change - **cambiar**	
To switch on - **encender**	
To switch off - **apagar**	
To switch over - **conmutar**	

S (cont.)

See Page

To swoon - **desmayar**
To swoop - **arrebatar**
To swop - **cambiar**
To symboloze - **simbolizar**
To sympathize - **simpatizar**
To synchronize - **sincronizar**
To syphon - **sacar con sifón** **94**

T

To table - **poner sobre la mesa** **77**
To tack *or* nail - **clavar**
To tack *(a boat)* - **virar**
To tackle - **atacar**
To tag - **marcar**
To tail *or* follow - **seguir** **47**
To tailor - **vestir** **112**
To taint - **manchar**
To take - **tomar** **93**
To take after - **parecerse** **84**
To take apart - **descomponer**
To take away - **llevar** **27**
To take back - **retractar**
To take care - **tener cuidado** **50/26**
To take care of - **cuidar de** **26**
To take charge of - **encargarse de**
To take delivery - **aceptar**
To take down - **abatir**
To take ill - **poner enfermo** **78**
To take notice - **notar**
To take off *(an aeroplane)* - **despegar**
To take off *(clothes)* -**desvestir**
To take out *(as one's purse etc.)* - **sacar** **94**
To take out *(on a date)* - **salir con** **48**
To take out *(as a tooth etc.)* - **extractar**
To take over - **tomar posesión** **93**
To take place - **tener efecto** **50**
To take something *or* someone somewhere - **llever** **27**
To talk - **hablar** **89**
To talk into - **persuadir**
To talk out of - **disuadir**
To talk over - **conversar**
To tame - **domesticar**
To tan *or* smack - **zurrar**
To tan *(in the sun)* - **broncear**
To tangle - **enredar**
To tantalize - **tentar**
To tap - **golpear ligeramente** **53**
To tap *(as a barrel etc.)* - **poner la espita** **77**
To tape together - **atar con cintas**

See Page

To tape record - **grabar en cinta magnetofónica**
To taper - **disminuar gradualmente**
To tar - **alquitranar**
To tarnish - **deslustrar**
To tarry - **tardar**
To taste *or* try - **probar** **95**
To have a taste - **tener sabor** **50**
To taste like *or* of - **saber de**
To taunt - **provocar**
To tax - **imponer impuestos**
To teach - **enseñar** **96**
To team up - **formar un equipo**
To team up with - **asociar**
To tear - **rasgar**
To tease - **tentar**
To teem - **vaciar**
To teethe - **endentecer**
To telegraph - **telegrafiar**
To telephone - **telefonear**
To telescope - **telescopar**
To tell - **decir** **82**
To tell off - **reñir**
To temper *(metal)* - **templar**
To tempt - **tentar**
To tend - **cuidar** **26**
To have a tendency to - **ir hacia** **46**
To tender *(offer)* - **ofrecer**
To tenderize - **hacer tierno** **32**
To terminate - **terminar** **41**
To terrace - **terraplenar**
To terrify - **aterrorizar**
To test - **probar** **95**
To testify - **testificar**
To tether - **trabar**
To thank - **agradecer**
To thaw - **deshelar**
To theorize - **teorizar**
To thicken - **espesar**
To thieve - **robar**
To grow thin - **adelgazar**
To thin out - **atenuar**
To think - **pensar** **97**
To thirst - **tener sed** **50**
To thrash - **azotar**
To thread - **enhebrar**
To threatem - **amenazar**
To thrill - **excitar**
To thrive - **prosperar**
To throb - **pulsar**
To throng - **atestar**
To throttle - **estrangular**
To throttle back - **reducir vueltas**

T (cont.)

	See Page
To throw - **tirar**	
To throw away or throw off - **desechar**	
To throw out - **echar**	74
To thrust - **empujar**	
To thrust aside, away or back - **rechazar**	
To thrust upon - **imponer**	
To thumb a lift - **hacer auto-stop**	
To thumb through - **hojear**	
To thump - **golpear**	53
To thunder - **tronar**	
To thwart - **frustrar**	
To tick - **sonar tictac**	
To tick over (a motor) - **andar en vacio**	
To tickle - **hacer cosquillas**	
To tidy - **arreglar**	13
To tie - **atar**	
To tighten - **apretar**	
To tile - **azulejar**	
To tile (a roof) - **tejar**	
To till - **cultivar**	
To tilt - **inclinar**	
To time - **tomar el tiempo de**	93
To tin or can - **enlatar**	
To tinge - **tinturar**	
To tingle - **sentir hormigueo**	39
To tinker with - **ocuparse vanamente con**	
To tinkle - **tintinear**	
To tint - **colorar**	
To tip (as a waiter etc.) - **dar propina**	
To tip off - **informar**	
To tip out - **echar**	74
To tip over - **volcar**	
To tip or tilt - **inclinar**	
To tipple - **beber**	33
To tiptoe - **andar de puntillas**	105
To tire - **cansar**	
To be tired - **estar cansado**	18
To tire out - **agotar**	
To titillate - **titilar**	
To title - **titular**	
To toast - **tostar**	
To toast (as the Queen etc.) - **brindar a la salud de**	
To toe the line - **conformarse**	
To toddle - **empezar andar**	20/105
To toil - **trabajar duro**	109
To tolerate - **tolerar**	
To toll - (as a bell) - **tañer**	
To tone with - **armonizar con**	
To top - **coronar**	
To top or better - **superar**	
To reach the top - **alcanzar la cima**	

	See Page
To top off or top out - **terminar**	41
To put topping - **cubrir**	
To top up - **llenar**	
To topple - **caer**	38
To make topple - **hacer caer**	32/38
To torment - **atormentar**	
To torpedo - **torpedear**	
To torture - **torturar**	
To toss - **tirar**	
To toss a coin - **lanzar una moneda al aire**	
To total - **totalizar**	
To totter - **tambalear**	
To touch - **tocar**	98
To touch down - **aterrizar**	
To toughen - **endurecer**	
To tour - **viajar**	100
To tout - **solicitar**	
To tow - **remolcar**	
To tower - **elevarse**	
To tower over - **sobresalir**	
To toy with - **jugar con**	73
To trace - **trazar**	
To trace back - **hacer remontar**	
To track or trail - **rastrear**	
To trade - **comerciar**	
To train - **enseñar**	96
To train (physically) - **entrenar**	
To tramp - **andar**	105
To trample - **pisotear**	
To transact - **tramitar**	
To transcend - **trascender**	
To transcribe - **transcribir**	
To transfer - **transferir**	
To transform - **transformar**	
To transgress - **infrigir**	
To translate - **traducir**	99
To transmit - **transmitir**	
To transpire - **transpirar**	
To transplant - **transplantar**	
To transport - **transportar**	
To trap - **atrapar**	
To travel - **viajar**	100
To traverse - **atravesar**	
To trawl - **pescar con red**	
To tread - **pisar**	
To treasure - **atesorar**	
To treat - **tratar**	
To treble - **triplicar**	
To tremble - **temblar**	
To trench - **atrincherar**	
To trend - **tender**	
To trespass - **traspasar**	

T (cont.)

	See Page
To trick - **engañar**	
To trickle - **escurrir**	
To trifle with - **jugar con**	73
To trim - **aparejar**	
To trim or prune - **podar**	
To trip - **tropezar**	
To triple or triplicate - **triplicar**	
To triumph - **triunfar**	
To trot - **trotar**	
To trouble - **molestar**	
To trust - **confiar**	
To try or taste - **probar**	95
To try to - **intentar**	101
To try on (clothes etc.) - **probar**	95
To tuck something in - **arropar**	
To tug - **arrastrar**	
To tumble - **caer**	38
To tune in - **sintonizar**	
To tune up - **ajustar**	
To tunnel - **hacer túnel**	32
To turn - **volver**	81
To turn around - **volver**	81
To turn away - **desviar**	
To turn back - **devolver**	81
To turn into - **convertir**	
To turn off (a light) - **apagar**	
To turn off (a tap) - **cerrar**	28
To turn on (a light) - **encender**	
To turn on (a tap) - **abrir**	70
To turn over (a page) - **hojear**	
To overturn - **volcar**	
To turn the corner - **doblar la esquina**	
To twang - **hacer vibrar**	32
To twin - **parear**	
To twinkle - **centellear**	
To twirl - **girar**	
To twist - **torcer**	
To twitch - **crispar**	
To twitter - **gorjear**	
To type or typewrite - **mecanografiar**	
To tyrannize - **tiranizar**	

U

	See Page
To ulcerate - **ulcerar**	
To umpire - **arbitrar**	
To unbend - **desencorvar**	
To unbuckle - **deshebillar**	
To unburden - **aliviar**	
To unburden oneself - **descargarse**	
To unbutton - **desabotonar**	
To uncoil - **desarollar**	
To uncork - **descorchar**	
To uncouple - **desconectar**	
To uncover - **descubrir**	
To undercut (prices) - **rebajar precios**	
To underestimate - **subestimar**	
To undergo - **sufrir**	
To underlay - **reforzar**	
To underlie - **formar la base de**	
To underline - **subrayar**	
To undermine - **zapar**	
To underpay - **pagar insuficiente**	72
To underrate - **menospreciar**	
To undersign - **firmar**	
To understand - **entender**	102
To undertake - **emprender**	
To undervalue - **subvalorar**	
To underwrite - **suscribir**	
To undo - **deshacer**	32
To undress - **desnudar**	
To undulate - **ondular**	
To unearth - **desenterrar**	
To unfasten - **desatar**	
To unfold or unfurl - **desplegar**	
To unhinge - **desengoznar**	
To unhook - **desenganchar**	
To unify - **unificar**	
To unite - **unir**	
To unlace - **desenlazar**	
To unload - **descargar**	
To unlock - **abrir**	70
To unmask - **desenmascara**	
To unnerve - **enervar**	
To unpack - **desempaquetar**	
To unpack (suitcases) - **deshacer las maletas**	
To unravel - **desenredar**	
To unroll - **desenrollar**	
To unscrew - **destornillar**	
To unseal - **abrir**	70
To unsettle - **trastornar**	
To unsheathe - **desenvainar**	
To untidy - **desarreglar**	13
To untie - **desatar**	
To unveil - **descubrir**	
To unveil (statues etc.) - **inaugurar**	
To unwrap - **desenvolver**	
To uphold - **mantener**	
To upholster - **tapizar**	
To uplift - **levantar**	
To uproot - **desarraigar**	
To upset - **trastornar**	
To upset or disarrange - **desarreglar**	13
To urge - **incitar**	

	See Page
To urinate - **orinar**	
To use - **usar**	103
To be used to - **soler**	
I am used to - **suelo**	
To use up - **consumir**	
To usher - **acomodar**	
To usurp - **usurpar**	
To utilize - **utilizar**	
To utter - **decir**	82

V

To vacate - **desocupar**	
To vaccinate - **vacunar**	
To vacillate - **vacilar**	
To value - **evaluar**	
To have value - **valer**	
To vanish - **desaparecer**	84
To vanquish - **vencer**	
To vaporize - **vaporizar**	
To varnish - **barnizar**	
To vary - **variar**	
To vault or jump - **saltar**	
To veer - **virar**	
To vegetate - **vegetar**	
To veil - **velar**	
To veneer - **chapear**	
To ventilate - **ventilar**	
To venture - **aventurar**	
To verify - **verificar**	
To veto - **vetar**	
To vex - **enfadar**	
To vibrate - **vibrar**	
To victimize - **hacer víctima**	32
To victual - **abastecer**	
To vie - **competir**	
To view - **mirar**	64
To vindicate - **vindicar**	
To violate - **violar**	
To visit - **visitar**	
To vitalize - **vitalizar**	
To vocalize - **vocalizar**	
To voice - **expresar**	
To volunteer - **ofrecerse**	
To vomit - **vomitar**	
To vote - **votar**	
To vouch for - **responder por**	
To vow - **hacer promesa**	32
To voyage - **viajar**	100
To vulcanize - **vulcanizar**	
To vulgarize - **vulgarizar**	

	See Page

W

To wad - **alcolchar**	
To waddle - **anadear**	
To wade - **vadear**	
To wag - **menear**	
To wage war - **guerrear**	
To wager - **apostar**	
To wail - **lamentar**	
To wait - **esperar**	104
To wait on - **servir**	
To waive - **renunciar**	
To wake up - **despertar**	
To walk - **andar**	105
To take a walk - **dar un paseo**	
To wall - **tapiar**	
To wallow - **revolcarse**	
To waltz - **bailar el vals**	
To wander - **vagar**	
To wane - **declinar**	
To want - **querer**	106
To war - **guerrear**	
To ward off - **desviar**	
To warm - **calentar**	
To warn - **advertir**	
To warp - **retorcer**	
To warp (wood) - **abangar**	
To warrant - **justificiar**	
To wash - **lavar**	107
To wash oneself - **lavarse**	108
To wash up - **fregar**	
To waste - **mal gastar**	
To waste away - **gastarse**	
To watch - **mirar**	64
To water - **regar**	
To wave - **saludar**	
To waver - **vacilar**	
To wax (polish) - **encerar**	
To waylay - **asechar**	
To weaken - **debilitar**	
To wear (clothes etc.) - **llevar**	27
To wear away, wear down or wear out - **gastar**	
To weary - **cansar**	
To weave - **tejer**	
To wed - **casar**	
To wedge - **calzar**	
To weed - **desherbar**	
To weep - **llorar**	
To weigh - **pesar**	
To weigh anchor - **desanclar**	
To welcome - **dar la bienvenido**	
To weld - **soldar**	

W (cont.)

	See Page
To wet - **mojar**	
To whack - **golpear**	**53**
To wheedle - **sonsacar**	
To wheel - **rodar**	
To whimper - **lloriquear**	
To whine - **gemir**	
To whip - **azotar**	
To whirl - **girar**	
To whisk away - **arrebatar**	
To whisk up - **batir**	
To whisper - **susurrar**	
To whistle - **silbar**	
To whiten or whitewash - **blanquear**	
To whiz - **zumbar**	
To whoop - **huchear**	
To widen - **ensanchar**	
To wield - **manejar**	
To will or want - **querer**	**106**
To will or leave to - **testar**	
To wilt - **ajar**	
To win - **ganar**	
To win (a battle) - **vencer**	
To wind (by turning) - **enrollar**	
To wind in and out - **serpentear**	
To be winded (out of breath) - **anhelar**	
To wine - **beber vino**	**33**
To wing or fly - **volar**	**42**
To wing or injure - **herir**	
To wink - **guiñar**	
To winter - **invernar**	
To wipe - **frotar**	
To wipe clean - **limpiar**	
To wire (electrical) - **alambrar**	
To wish or wish for - **querer**	**106**
To withdraw - **retirar**	
To wither - **ajar**	
To withhold - **retener**	**54**
To withstand - **resistir**	
To witness - **presenciar**	
To bear witness - **testificar**	
To wobble - **tambalear**	
To wonder - **especular**	
or to ask oneself - **preguntarse**	**15**
To woo - **cortejar**	
To word - **expresar**	
To work - **trabajar**	**109**
To work (a machine) - **functionar**	
To worry - **preocupar**	
To worry oneself - **preocuparse**	
To worry someone else - **molestar**	
To worsen - **empeorar**	
To worship - **adorar**	
To be worth - **valer**	
To wound - **herir**	
To wrangle - **disputar**	
To wrap - **envolver**	
To wreck - **destruir**	
To wreck (a ship) - **naufragar**	
To wrench - **arrancar**	
To wrestle - **luchar**	
To wriggle - **menear**	
To wriggle out of - **escurrirse**	
To wring - **torcer**	
To wrinkle - **arrugar**	
To write - **escribir**	**110**

X

	See Page
To x-ray - **radiografiar**	

Y

	See Page
To yacht - **viajar en yate**	**100**
To yank - **tirar**	
To yawn - **bostezar**	
To yearn - **anhelar**	
To yell - **gritar**	
To yellow - **amarillecer**	
To yelp - **gañir**	
To yield (produce) - **producir**	
To yield (give way) - **ceder**	
To yodel - **cantar**	
To yoke - **enyugar**	

Z

	See Page
To zero - **poner a cero**	**77**
To zigzag - **zigzaguar**	
To zip - **zumbar**	
To zip up - **cerrar con cremallera**	**28**
To un-zip - **abrir la cremallera**	**70**
To zone - **dividir**	
To zoom - **zumbar**	

Learning a language is very much an on going thing. You will reach a stage where you are able to express yourself but have difficulty in understanding what is being said to you. You will find that some people you understand quite easily and others with difficulty or not at all, this can be due to regional variation of dialect or just the fact that some people speak their own language very badly! By this I mean that not everyone has had the benefit of elocution lessons or has good diction, and whereas some people will speak to you slowly and clearly, others unfortunately, will speak quickly and indistinctly.